CARICATURES

GENE MARKEY
Ether Editors

ETHER EDITIONS

CONTENTS

CARICATURES

FOREWORD

Before the thoroughbred racehorses and Kentucky's Calumet Farm, before his distinguished service with the United States Navy during the Second World War, before his successful career as a Hollywood producer and screenwriter and his several less-than-successful Hollywood marriages, Gene Markey was a caricaturist, and a very good one.

Early in his long and varied career, Gene Markey drew a series of caricatures that captured the idiosyncrasies of America's literary and theatrical celebrities and other newsworthy characters of the early 1920s. His subjects included actors, critics, musicians, newspaper editors, poets, professors, and writers. Some of these characters achieved enduring fame, while others are now largely forgotten, but Gene Markey's caricatures make them all seem curiously familiar.

Eugene Willford "Gene" Markey (1895-1980) was born December 11th in Jackson, Michigan and grew up in nearby Battle Creek, where his father, former United States Army Colonel Eugene Lawrence Markey, was a successful executive with the Duplex Printing Press Company. The Markey family lived a comfortable life on Chestnut Street in Battle Creek, where the young Markey attended Central High School. After graduation, Markey left Michigan for New Hampshire and Dartmouth College. At Dartmouth, he and his fellow classmates produced amateur theatricals for the Dartmouth Dramatic Association and the Dartmouth Players. Gene Markey would go on to graduate with the Dartmouth Class of 1918 after serving briefly in the United States Army during the First World War.

After the war, Markey moved to Chicago, where he attended the School of the Chicago Art Institute. He joined the recently inaugurated membership organization The Bookfellows (member #1121), which styled itself as "An International Association of Readers and Writers." Several members of The Bookfellows would eventually find themselves caricatured by Markey, including James Branch Cabell, Clarence Darrow, Hamlin Garland, Carl Sandburg, Vincent Starrett, and Hugh Walpole. The Bookfellows published The Step Ladder, where some of Markey's first sketches appeared.

While living in Chicago, Gene Markey freelanced for newspapers and magazines, writing the occasional literary critique or short story, and illustrating the literary pages of various publications, including the Chicago Daily News and the New York Tribune. His work with the Chicago Daily News eventually gained the young Markey entrée to Chicago's literary circle and its preferred haunt, Schlogl's Restaurant on Wells Street. The festive gatherings at Schlogl's in Chicago have often been compared to similar goings-on at New York's Algonquin Round Table.

In Midwest Portraits, a memoir of the period, the journalist and historian Harry Hansen (caricatured herein) characterized the young Gene Markey as "a critic who has led readers to books." As Markey's caricatures appeared more frequently in the popular press, they soon came to the attention of book publishers. Gene Markey's first volume of caricatures, entitled Literary Lights, was published in New York by Alfred A. Knopf in 1923. The Chicago publishers Covici-McGee brought out Markey's next book, a more Chicago-oriented collection entitled Men About Town, in 1924. Gene Markey's caricatures from these two publications, with the original captions he appended to them, are collected in the present volume.

During his time in Chicago, Markey also worked on his writing skills. His short stories began to appear in various publications, including The Blue Book, The Bookman, Harper's Bazaar, Scribner's Magazine, and The Wave, the latter a short-lived periodical edited by Vincent Starrett. Gene Markey must have been bitten by the Hollywood bug when he sold his story "Blinky" to Universal Pictures. "Blinky," a western tale, was filmed in 1923 with Hoot Gibson in the starring role. Gibson was then among the Hollywood actors making the transition from the silents to the talkies. By the end of the decade, Gene Markey would begin making a transition of his own, from a Chicago-based caricaturist and short-story writer to a successful Hollywood screenwriter and producer.

Ambitious, energetic, and socially adroit, Gene Markey was a natural in Hollywood. Once established in the rapidly growing movie capital of America, Markey would go on to serve as associate producer, producer, scenarist, or screenwriter on dozens of films. Those on which he is credited as original writer or screenwriter include "Syncopation" (1929) with Morton Downey and Barbara Bennett from his novel Stepping High, "A Modern Hero" with Richard Barthelmess and Jean Muir (1934), and "Private Number" with Robert Taylor and Loretta Young (1936). He assumed the role of Associate Producer on the Shirley Temple vehicles "Wee Willie Winkie" (1937) and "The Little Princess" (1939), as well as on "The Hound of the Baskervilles" (1939) and "The Adventures of Sherlock Holmes" (1939), both starring Basil Rathbone.

The Second World War put Gene Markey's Hollywood career on hold, but he did not hesitate to serve. Markey had become a naval reservist after his service in the Army during the First World War, and when war broke out again in Europe and America subsequently entered the conflict, he returned to active service in the United States Navy. Markey served in the Pacific under the command of Admiral "Bull" Halsey.

While Gene Markey spent his Hollywood career off-screen, he did provide the inspiration for at least one on-screen performance. The novelist James Bassett, author of the World War II naval epic Harm's Way, based his character Egan Powell on Gene Markey. Bassett and Markey both served under Admiral Halsey in the Pacific. When Bassett's novel was filmed by director Otto Preminger as "In Harm's Way," Egan Powell was played by the renowned character actor Burgess Meredith. At one point in Bassett's story, Egan Powell advises the lead character Rockwell Torrey, played in the Preminger film by John Wayne, to never (emphasis added) marry an actress. The advice was certainly telling and perhaps a bit of an inside joke. During the 1930s and 1940s, Markey was married to three of Hollywood's most celebrated leading ladies, including Joan Bennett (1932-1937), Hedy Lamaar (1939-1941), and Myrna Loy (1946-1950). Each of these Hollywood marriages ended in divorce.

During the early 1950s, sometime after this third marriage ended, Gene Markey met Lucille Parker Wright, the recently widowed owner of Calumet Farm, the legendary thoroughbred horse racing operation in Lexington, Kentucky. Upon his subsequent marriage to Lucille, Markey left Hollywood behind and assumed the role of country squire, joining his fourth wife in the exclusive world of prize-winning thoroughbred horse racing, a world that Hollywood had always found alluring. During his years at Calumet Farm, Gene Markey wrote several popular novels, including Kentucky Pride and That Far Paradise. Witty and urbane, and known to mix a superlative cocktail, Gene Markey brought a new sense of life to Calumet. He and the new Mrs. Markey must have been a good match. The two would spend the rest of their lives together.

Gene Markey's life is the stuff of Hollywood legend and fertile ground for the attentions of a modern biographer. While such a study is beyond the scope of the present work, no story of Gene Markey's life and career, in Hollywood and elsewhere, would be complete without due consideration of his early talent as a caricaturist.

LITERARY LIGHTS

LITERARY LIGHTS

Hamlin Garland

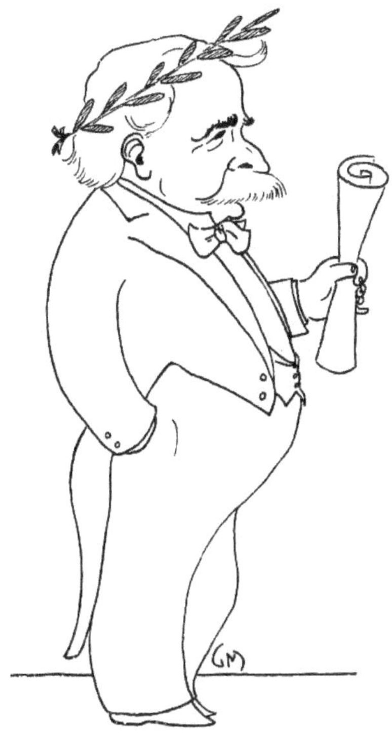

Hamlin Garland, crowned by the Académie Américaine.

Joseph Hergesheimer

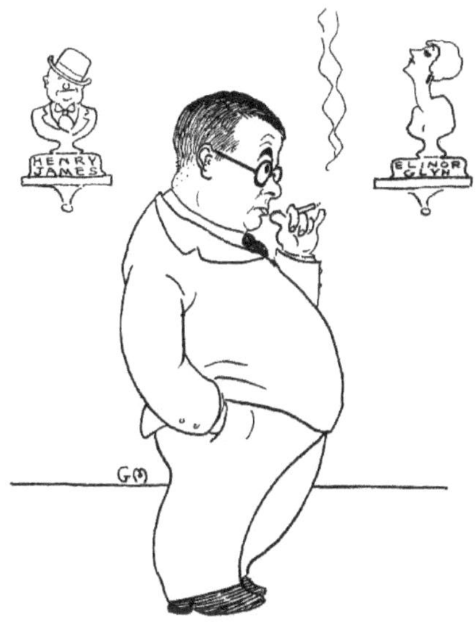

Joseph Hergesheimer: The author of Cytherea (according to a reviewer in Jonesville, Arkansas) considers two pronounced literary influences.

Sherwood Anderson

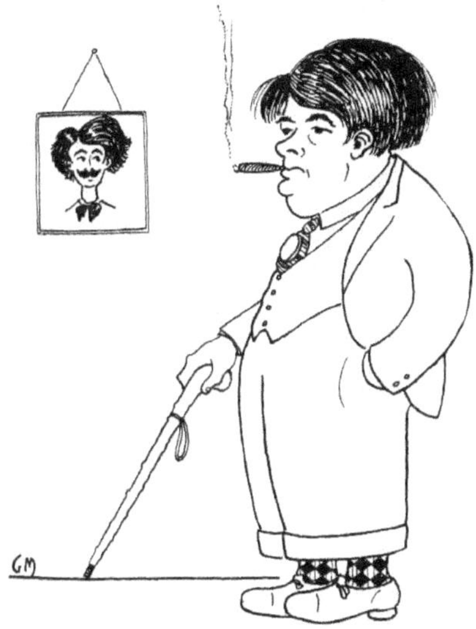

Sherwood Anderson wondering if the report be true
that he is a greater realist than Zola.

Henry Kitchell Webster

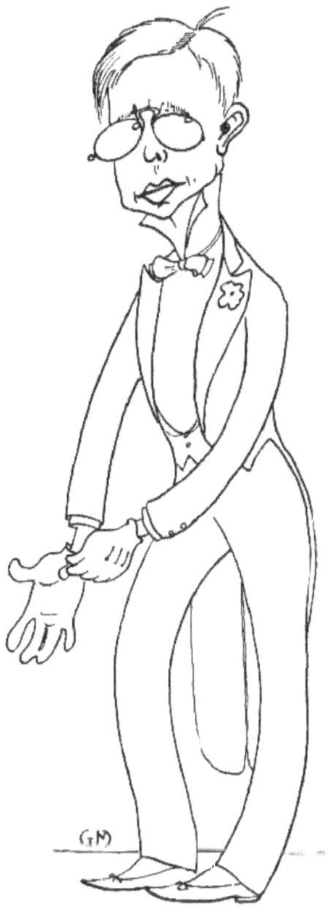

Henry Kitchell Webster, getting ready for a hard night at the Opera.

John Dos Passos and F. Scott Fitzgerald

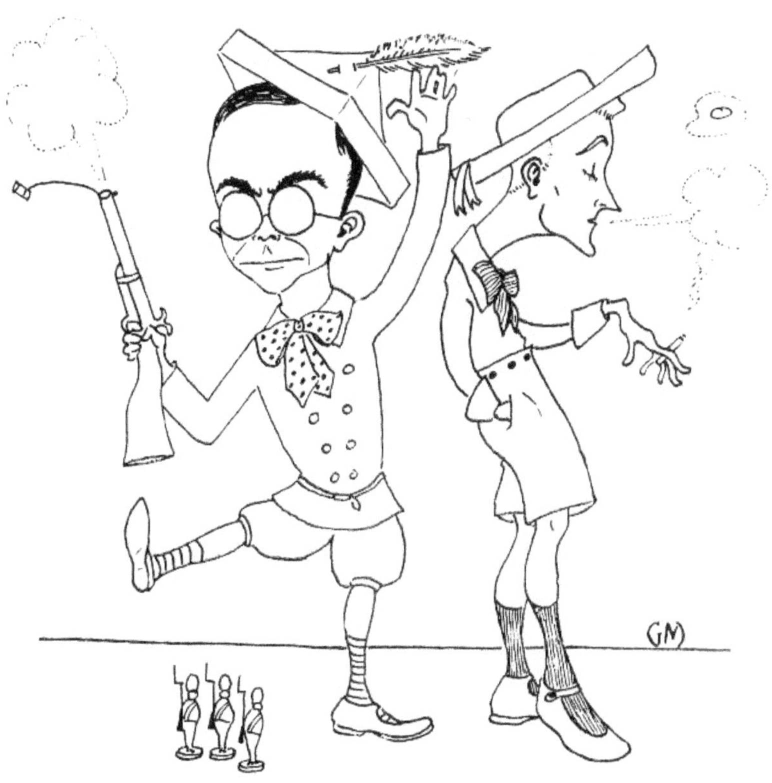

Les Enfants Terribles: John Dos Passos and F. Scott Fitzgerald.

Christopher Morley

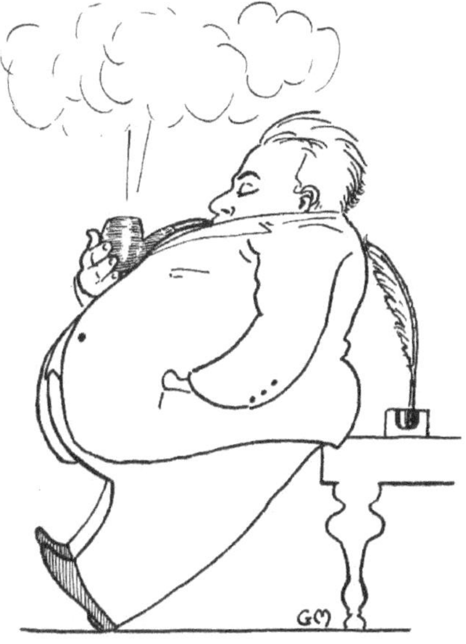

Christopher Morley about to write an Essay.

Carl Sandburg

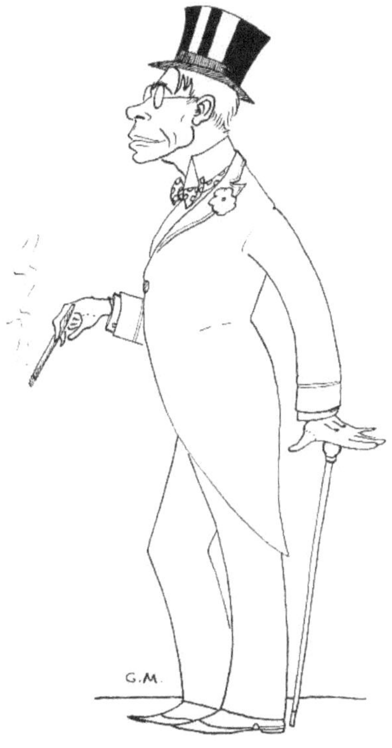

Carl Sandburg calls upon The Poetry Society of America.

Theodore Dreiser and E. Phillips Oppenheim

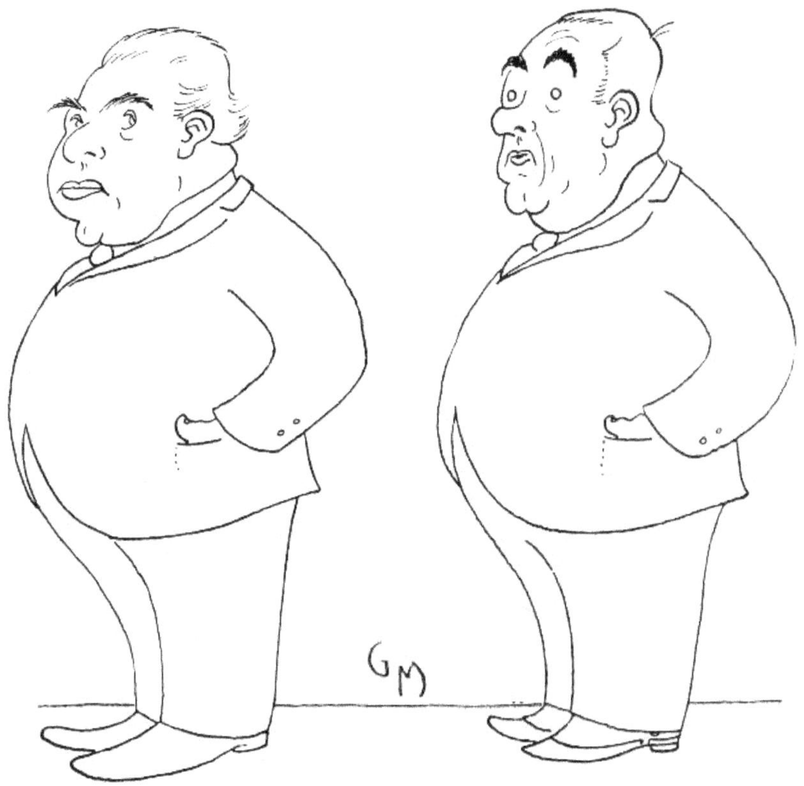

Two Great Realists: Theodore Dreiser and E. Phillips Oppenheim.

Edgar Lee Masters

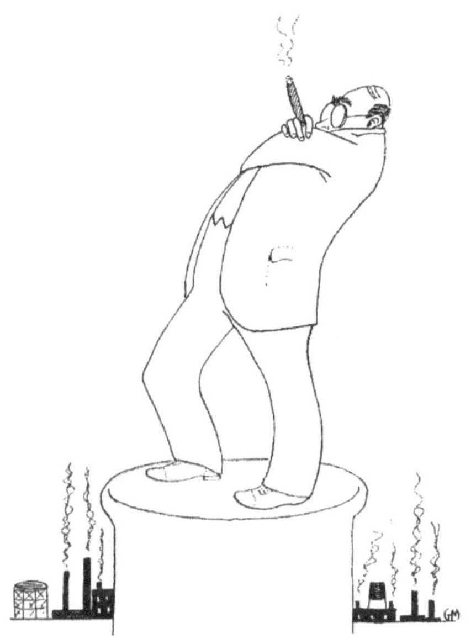

Edgar Lee Masters, at mention of Chicago as a literary capital, contemplates flight to Italy.

Donald Ogden Stewart and Louis Untermeyer

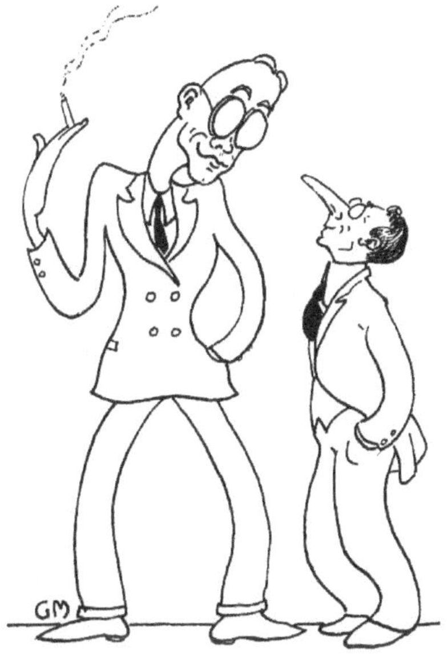

A Pair of Parodists: Donald Ogden Stewart and Louis Untermeyer.

Don Marquis

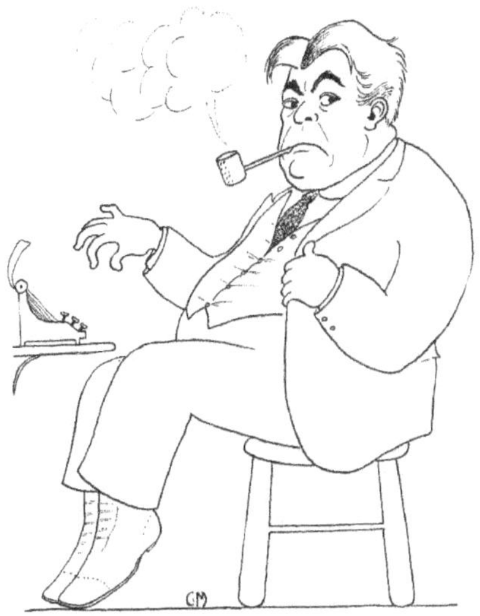

Don Marquis composing a Sonnet.

Zane Grey, Emerson Hough, and Philip Ashton Rollins

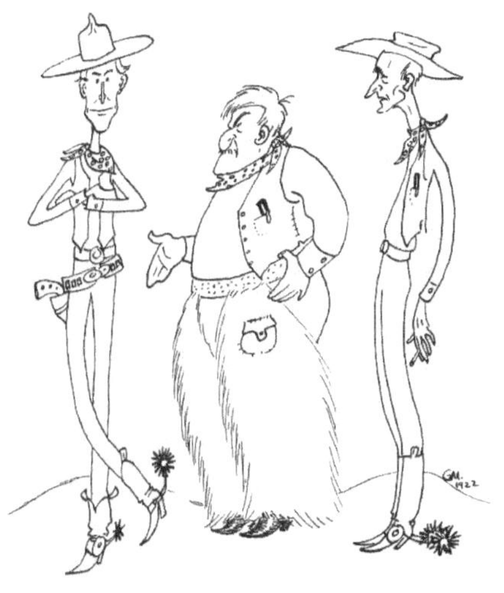

Zane Grey, Emerson Hough, and Philip Ashton Rollins discuss western fiction.

Ben Hecht

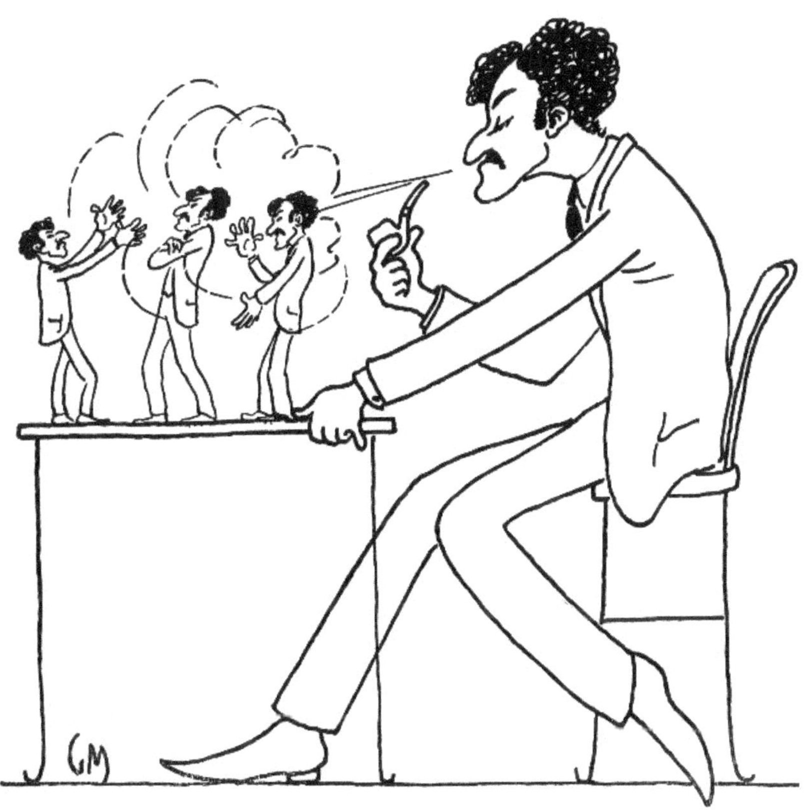

Ben Hecht and some of the characters in Erik Dorn.

Heywood Broun

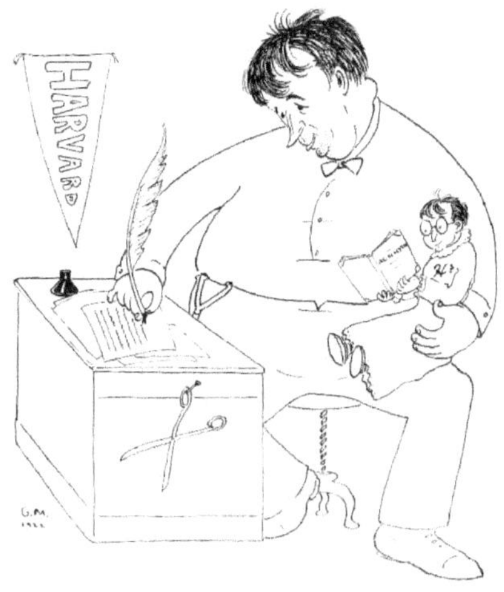

Heywood Broun, blighting an entire crop of spring novels.

Charles Hanson Towne

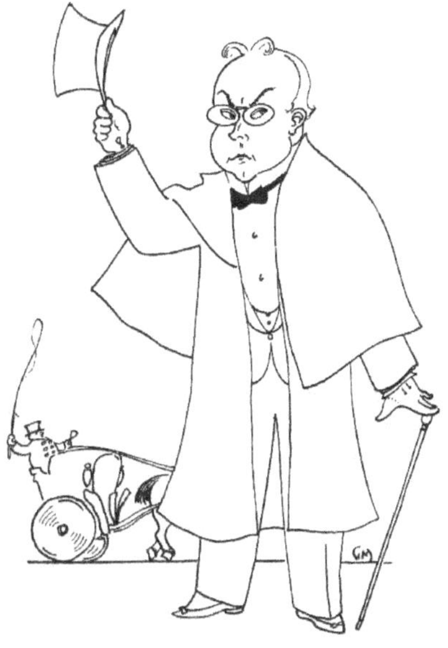

One of the characters in Charles Hanson Towne's novel.

John Weaver and John C. Farrar

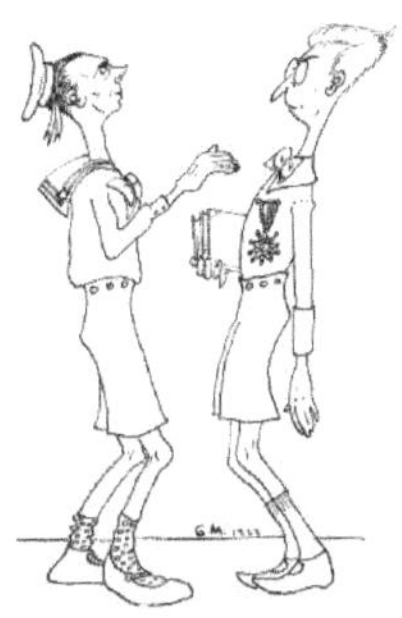

*Johnny Weaver conferring upon Johnny Farrar
the Order of the Brooklyn Eagle.*

Robert Cortes Holliday

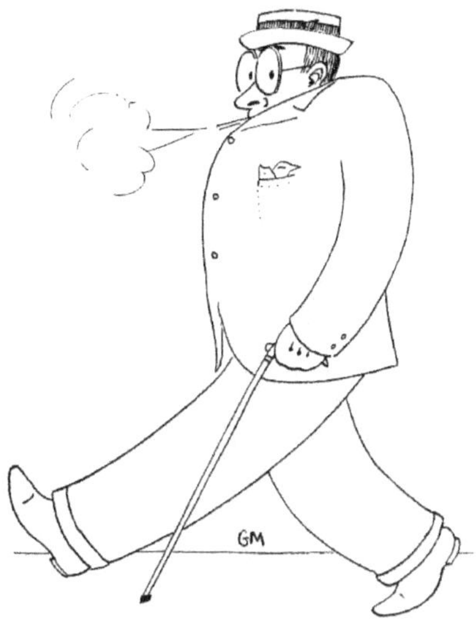

Robert Cortes Holliday and his famous Walking-Stick.

H. L. Mencken and Hugh Walpole

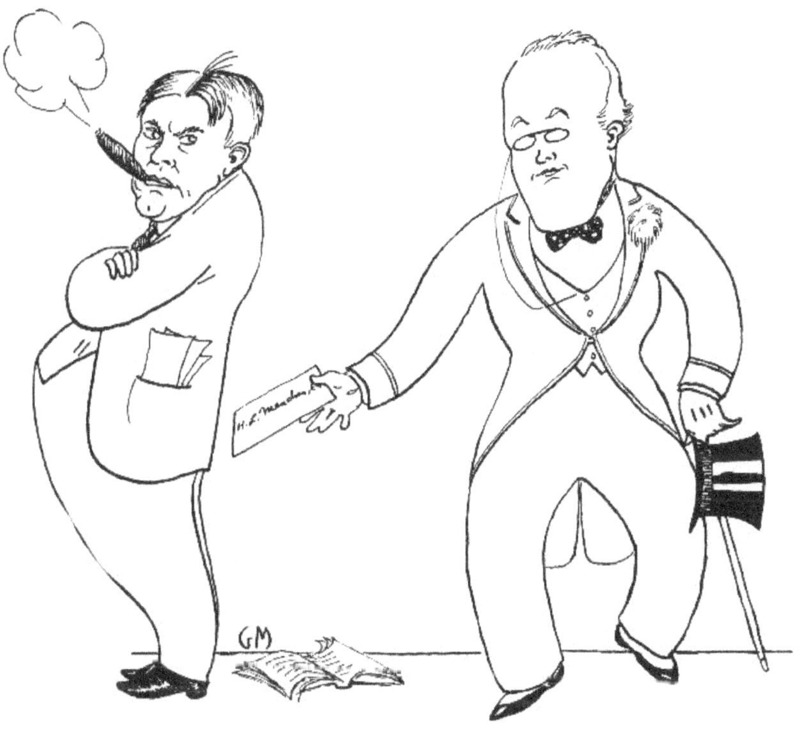

An Invitation: Hugh Walpole invites Mr. Mencken to England.

William Allen White

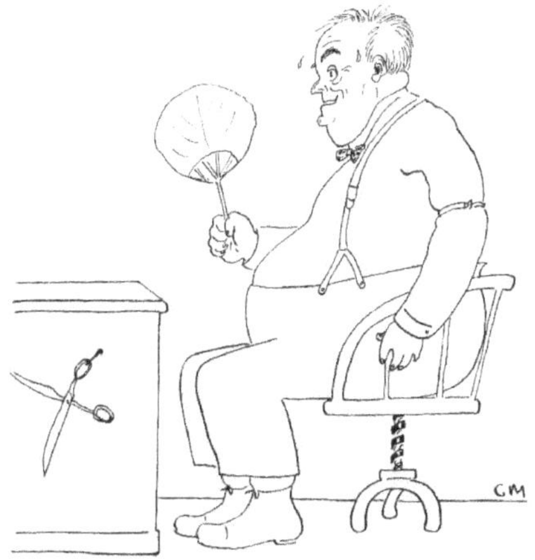

The Sage of Kansas: William Allen White.

Ernest Boyd

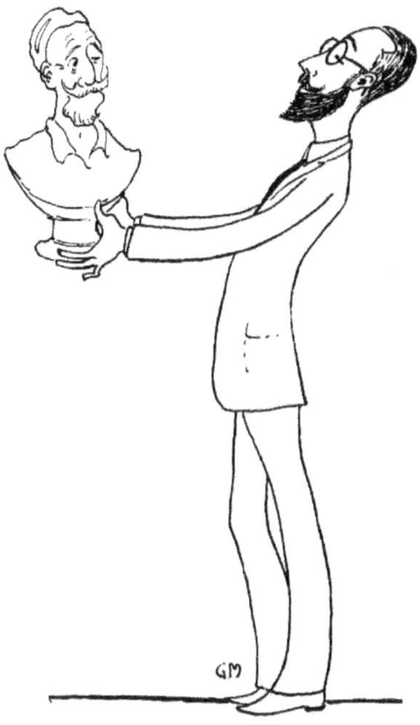

Ernest Boyd and the master [Anatole France].

Keith Preston, Richard Henry Little, and Richard Atwater

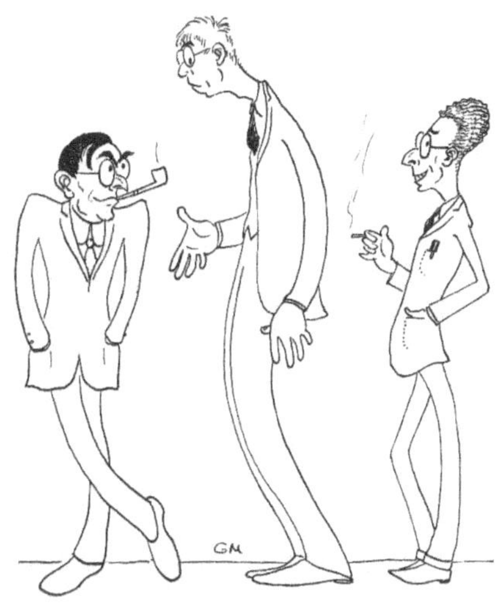

Three Chicago Columnists: Keith Preston, Richard Henry Little, and Richard Atwater ("Riq.").

Henry Sell

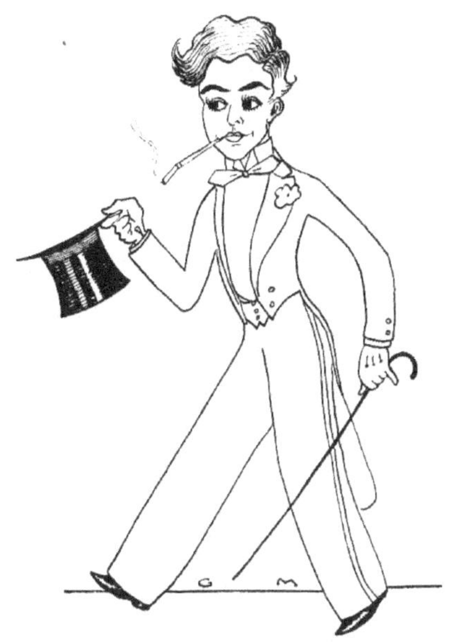

Henry Sell enters the Ritz.

Harrison Rhodes

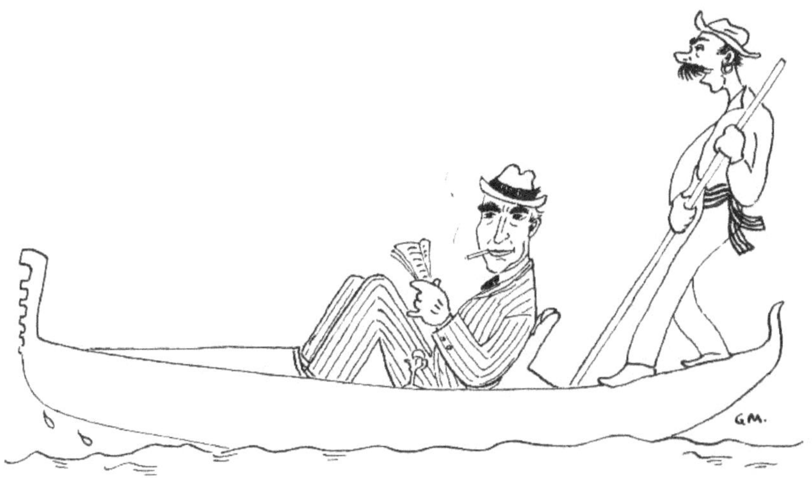

Harrison Rhodes takes the air in Venice.

Maxwell Bodenheim and
Edgar A. Guest

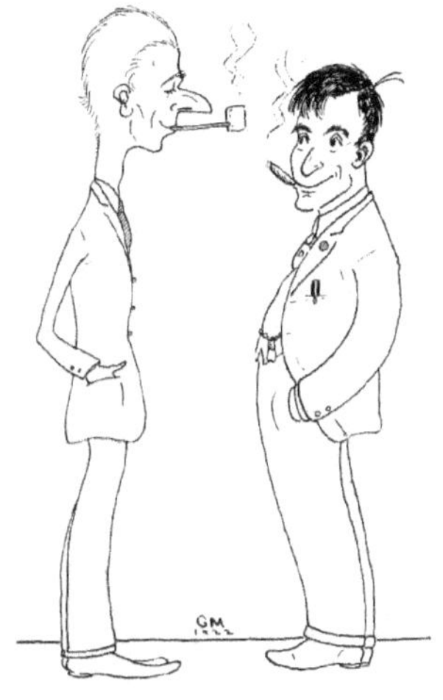

Imaginary Conversations: Maxwell Bodenheim and Edgar A. Guest.

Harry Hansen

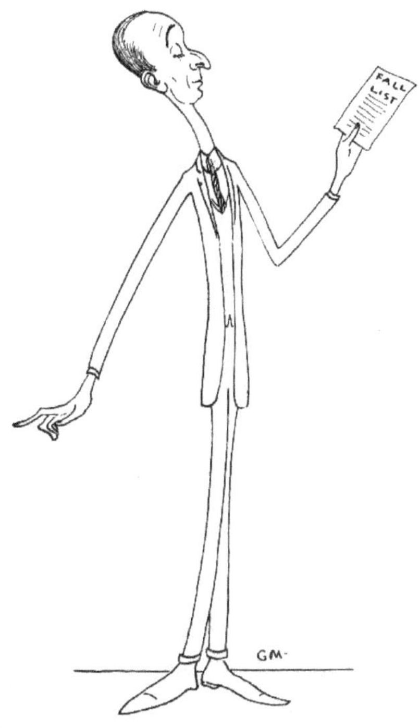

Harry Hansen glances over a publisher's list.

Burton Rascoe

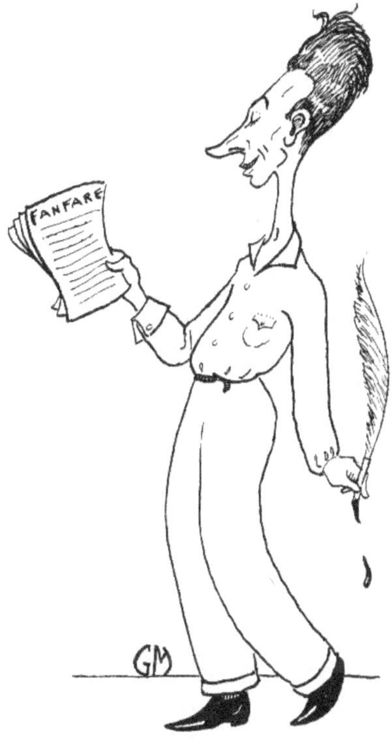

Burton Rascoe looks with favor upon a Manuscript.

Llewellyn Jones

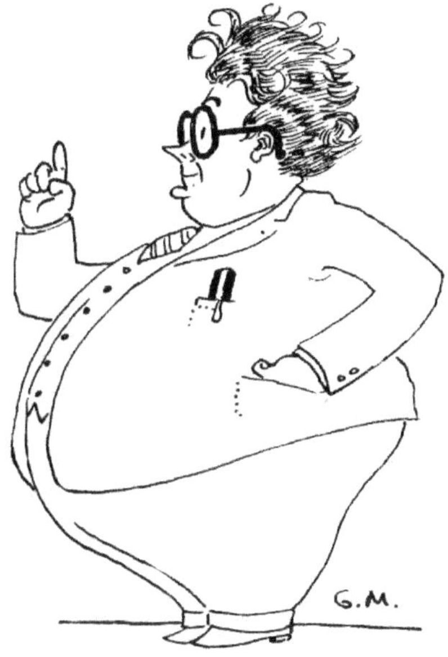

Llewellyn Jones contemplates a four-column article,
annihilating a group of New England Poets.

Stephen Vincent Benet and William Rose Benet

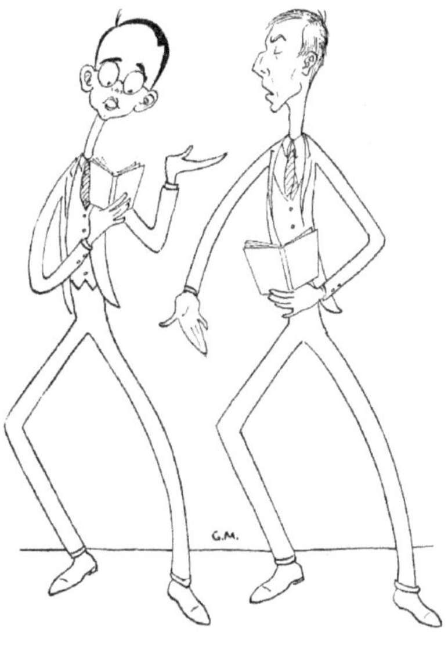

The Brothers Benet read to each other from their own works.

Karl Edwin Harriman

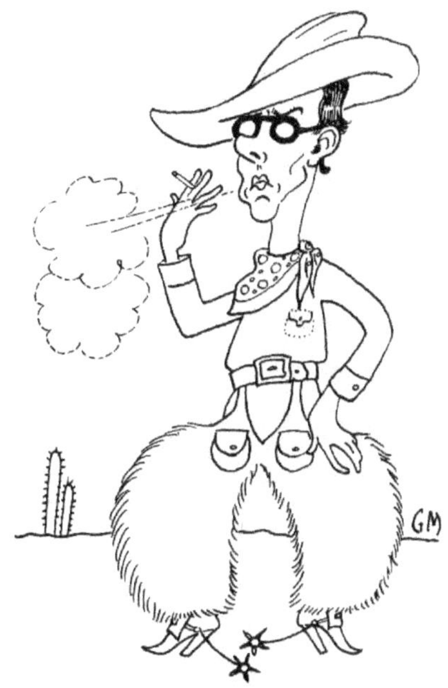

Karl Edwin Harriman: The Editor of The Red Book in the West on a hunting trip — hunting for western stories.

James Branch Cabell

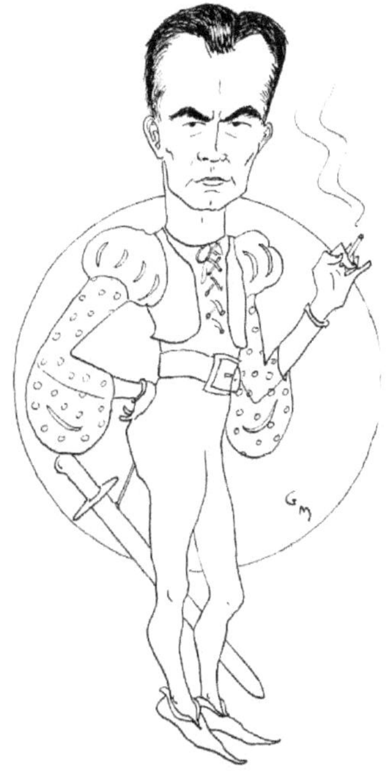

James Branch Cabell.

Franklin Pierce Adams

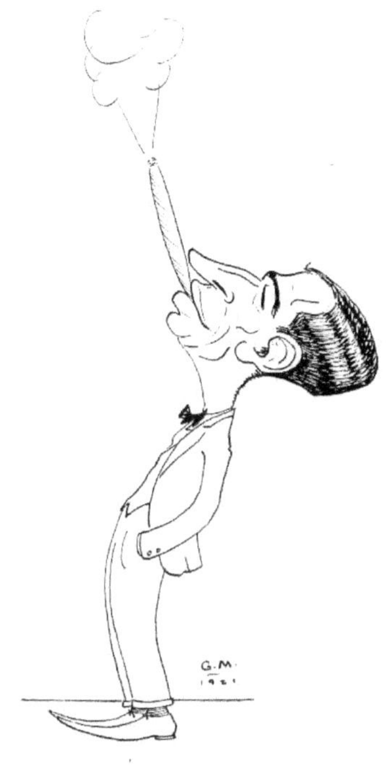

F. P. A. [Franklin Pierce Adams].

Carl Van Vechten

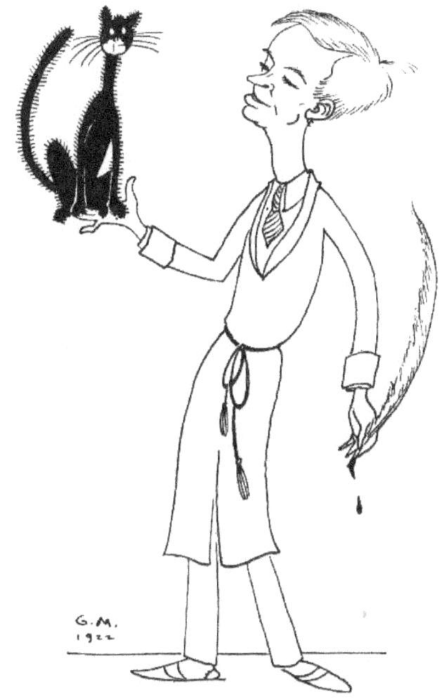

Carl Van Vechten plans another book.

Hendrik Willem Van Loon

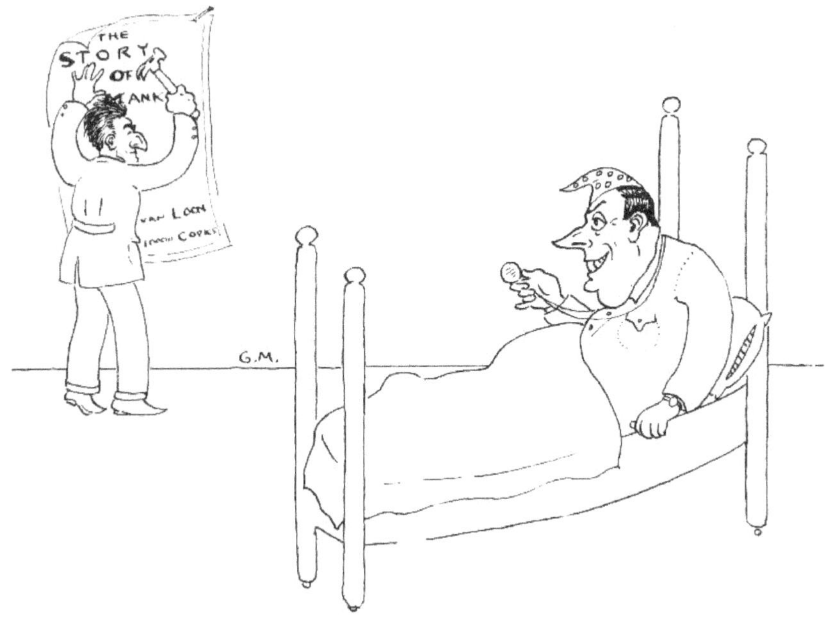

Hendrik Willem Van Loon wakes up to find himself famous.

Vincent Starrett

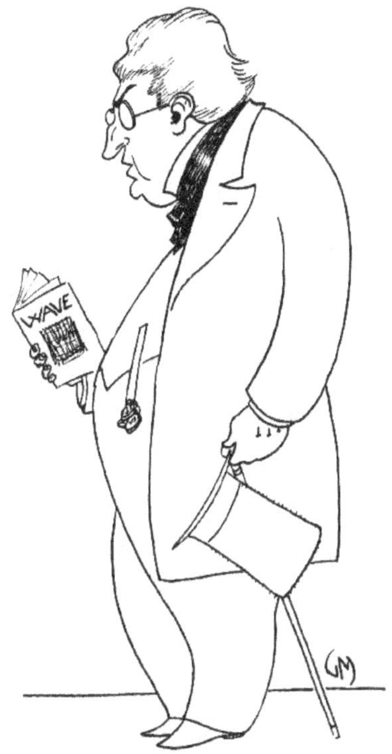

An Eminent Victorian. Vincent Starrett: "What is the wild Wave saying?"

A. Edward Newton

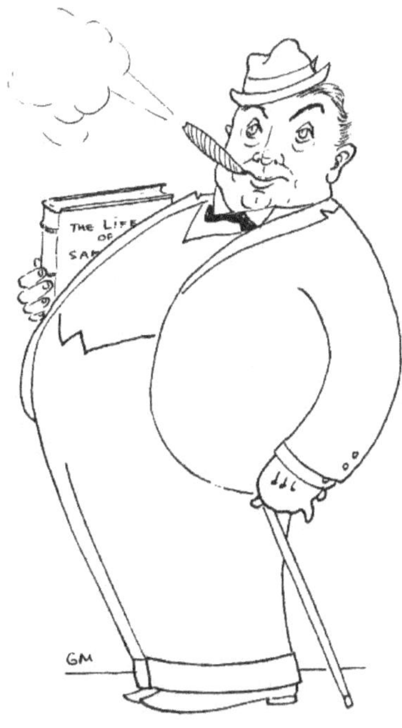

An Eminent Johnsonian: A. Edward Newton, Esq.

Robert C. Benchley, Percy Hammond, and Alexander Woollcott

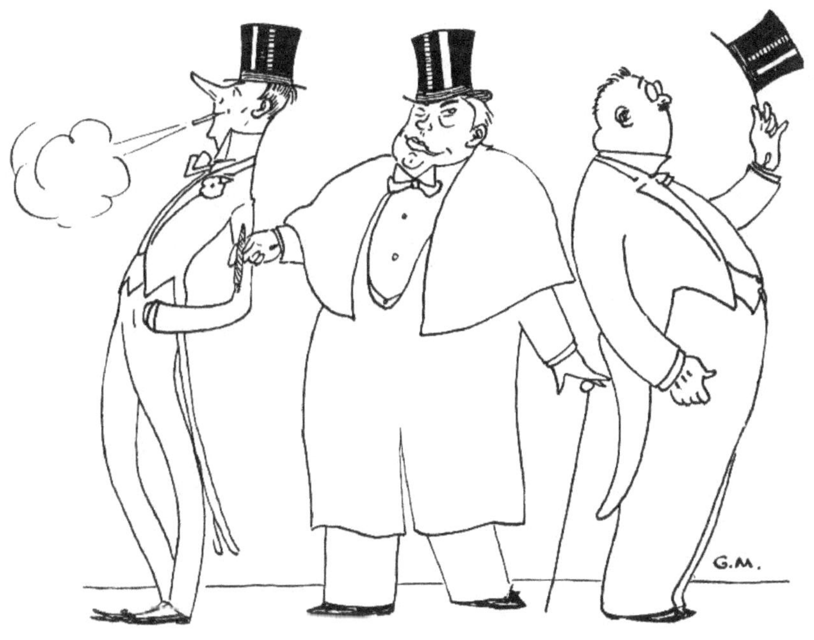

Three New York Drama Critics: Robert C. Benchley, Percy Hammond, and Alexander Woollcott.

Charles Collins, Ashton Stevens and O. L. Hall

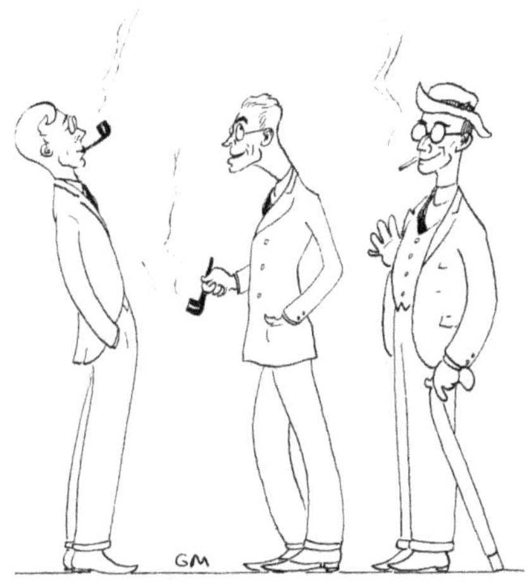

Three Chicago Drama Critics: Charles Collins,
Ashton Stevens and O. L. Hall.

George Jean Nathan

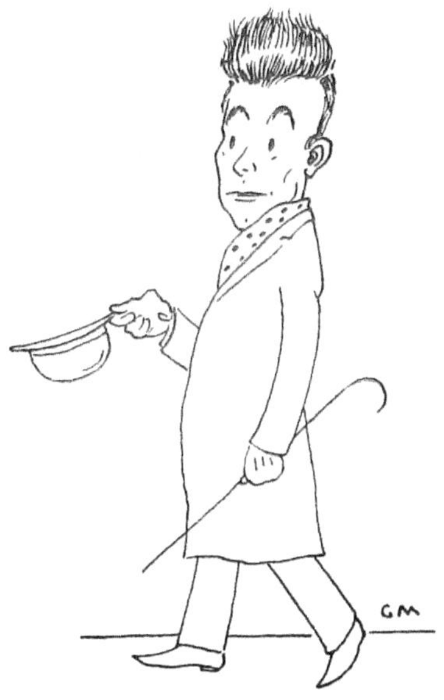

Mr. Nathan goes to the play.

Charles Crane and Thomas Beer

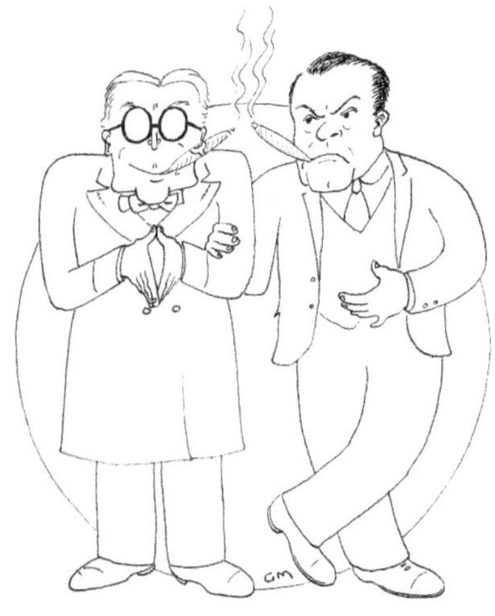

Imaginary Conversations: Dr. Charles Crane and Thomas Beer.

H. L. Mencken

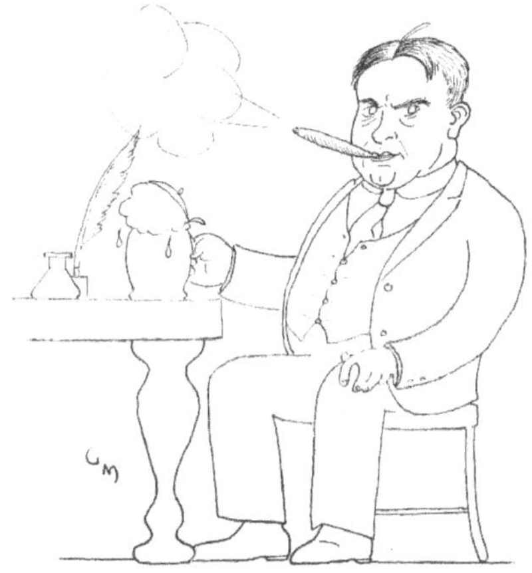

H. L. Mencken trying to think of more things that annoy him.

Sinclair Lewis

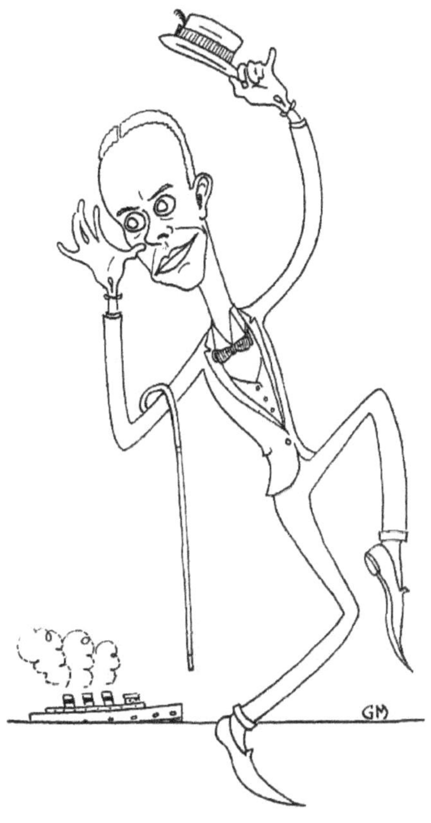

A Gesture of Farewell: Sinclair Lewis returns from England.

William Lyon Phelps

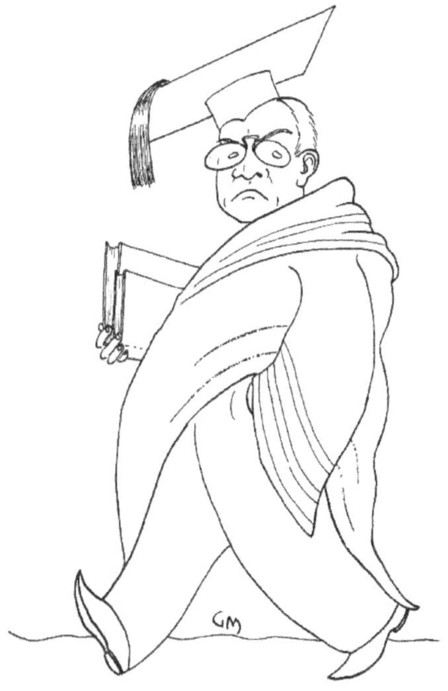

Prof. William Lyon Phelps, in an un-academic moment,
strolls homeward with an eclectic assortment of autumn novels.

Keith Preston

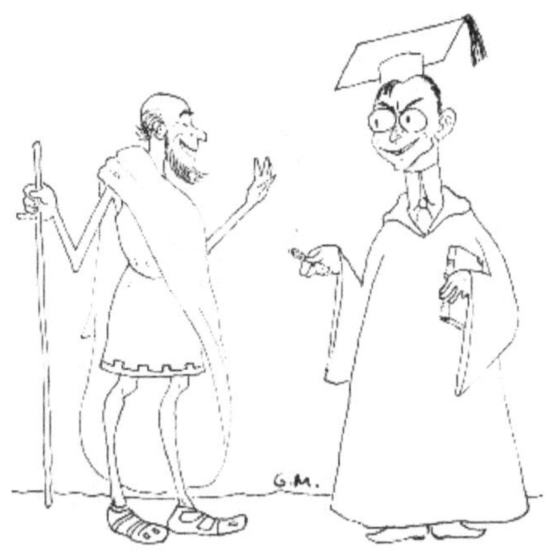

Keith Preston cracks a quip with the Shade of Petronius.

John Drew

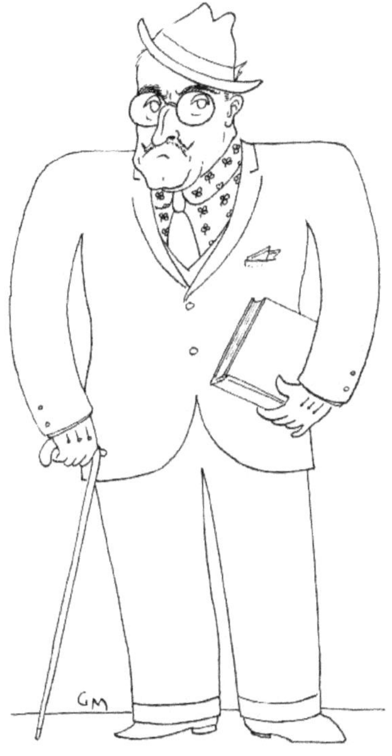

John Drew brings forth his memoirs.

John Peale Bishop and Edmund Wilson

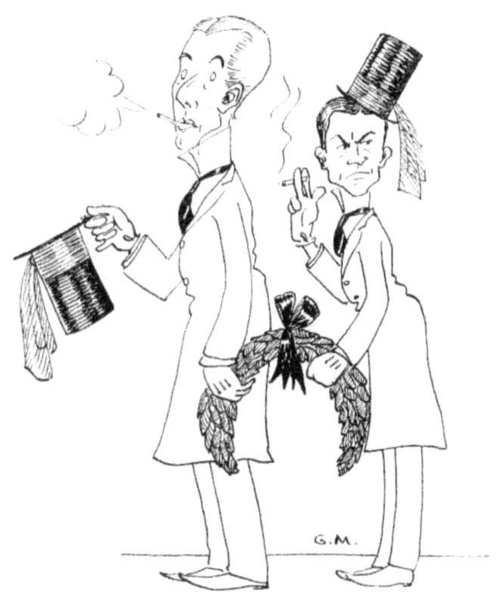

John Peale Bishop and Edmund Wilson Jr.
bring forth The Undertaker's Garland.

Booth Tarkington

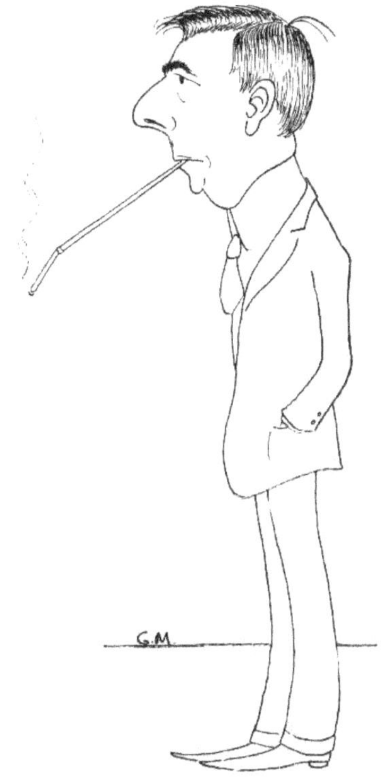

MR. TARKINGTON.

Achmed Abdullah and Edwin Balmer

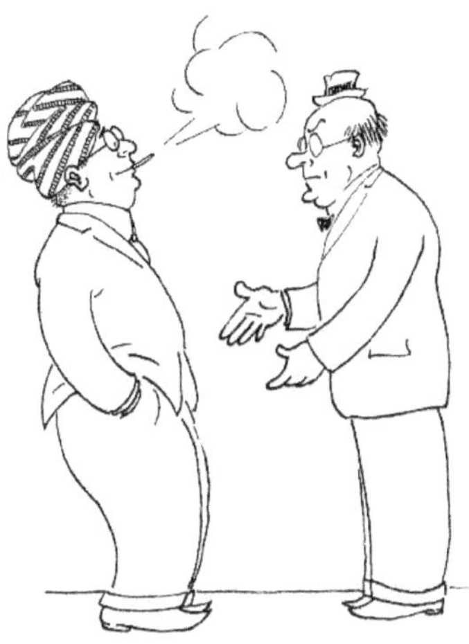

Cosmopolitan: Achmed Abdullah and Edwin Balmer.

Frederick O'Brien

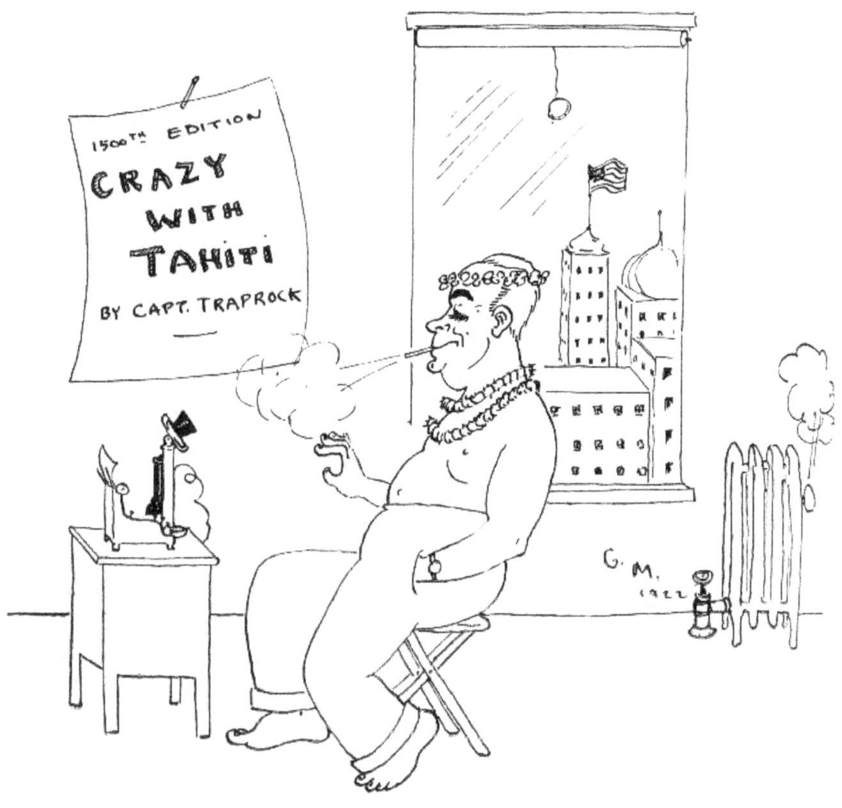

Frederick O'Brien contemplates the 86th volume
of his chaste adventures in the South Seas.

John Collings Squire and Carl Sandburg

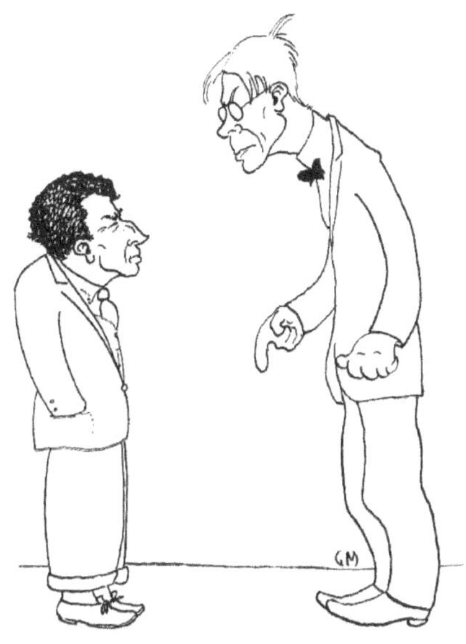

J. C. Squire and Carl Sandburg revive the ancient Whistler-Ruskin Controversy.

Stuart P. Sherman

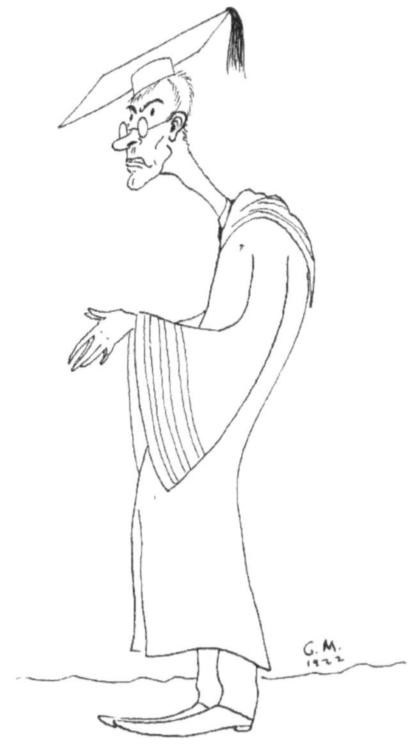

*Prof. Stuart P. Sherman meditates upon
the shocking state of American Letters.*

MEN ABOUT TOWN

Arthur Aldis

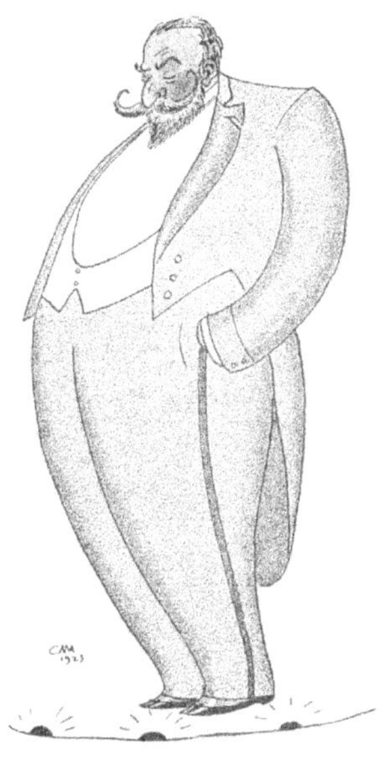

Mr. Arthur Aldis introducing a distinguished foreign visitor.

Sherwood Anderson

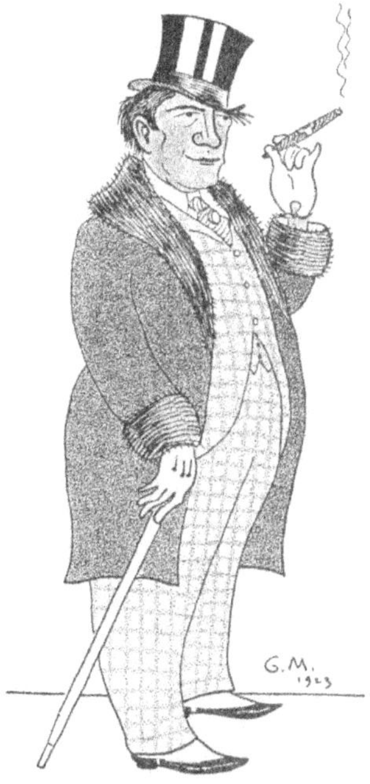

Mr. Sherwood Anderson discovers that he is a best-seller.

J. Ogden Armour

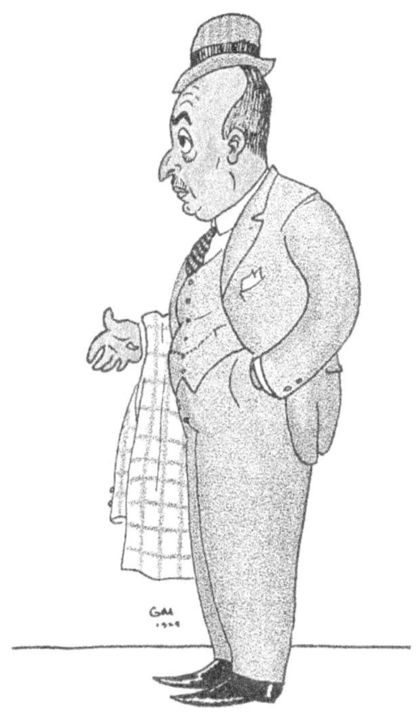

Mr. J. Ogden Armour looks up an early sailing for Europe.

Richard Atwater

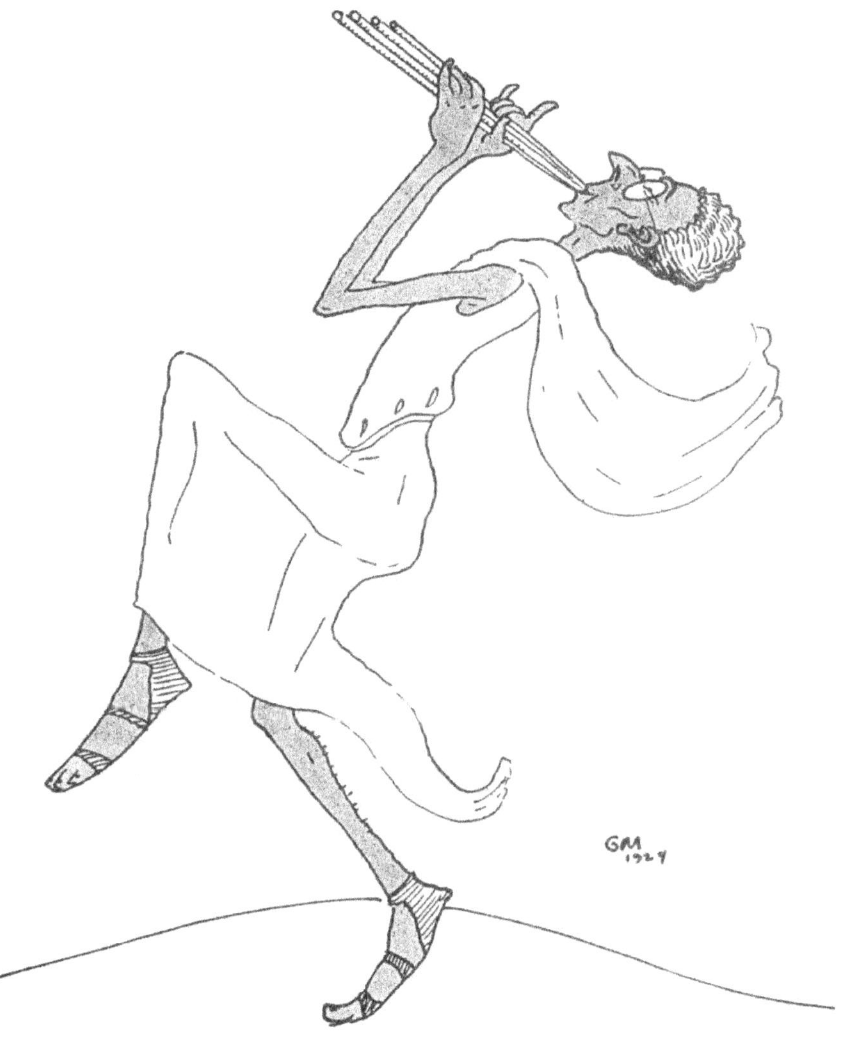

Mr. Riquarius Atwater spends a week-end on the Dunes.

Edwin Balmer

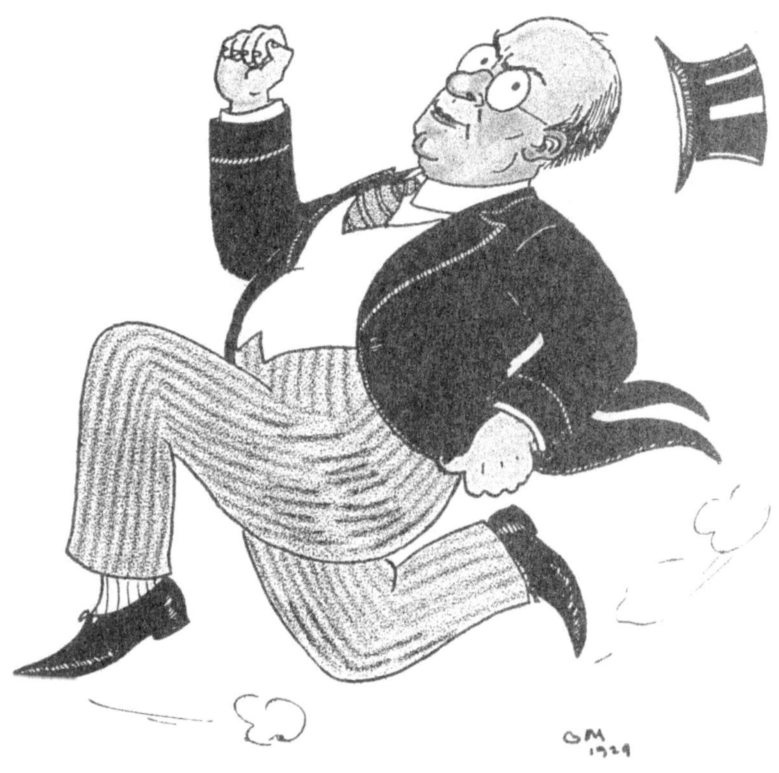

Mr. Edwin Balmer takes a quiet stroll in Evanston.

Maxwell Bodenheim

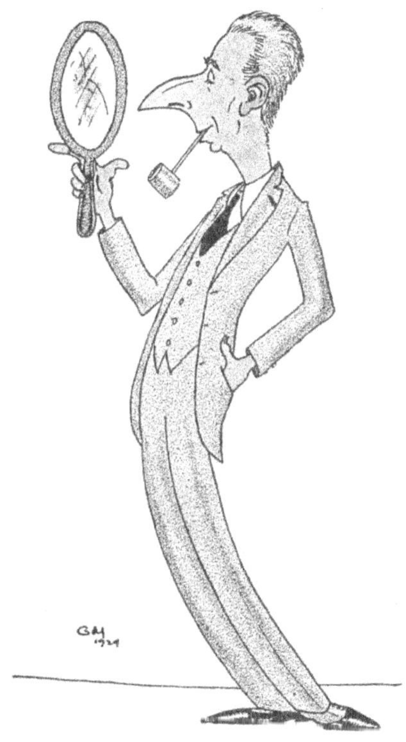

Mr. Maxwell Bodenheim meets his favorite poet.

Sheppard Butler

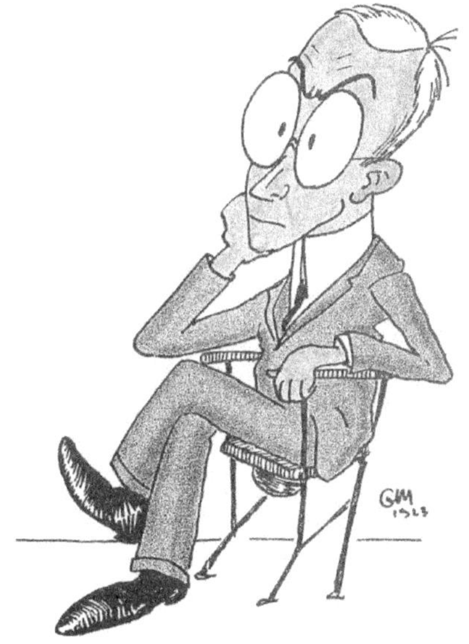

Mr. Sheppard Butler in an attitude of enjoying or not enjoying a play.

Ernest L. Byfield and Eugene Byfield

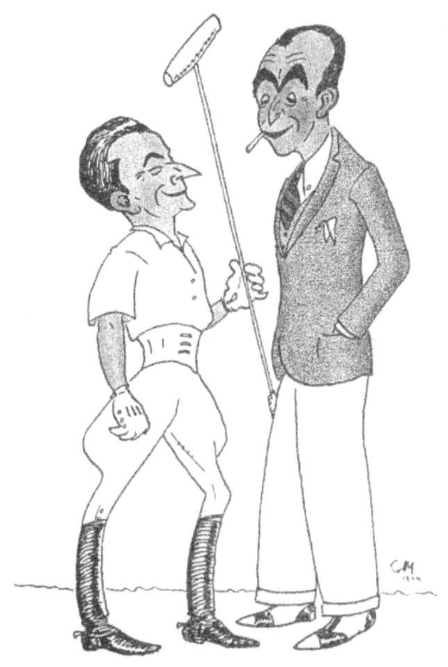

The Brothers Byfield.

John Allen Carpenter

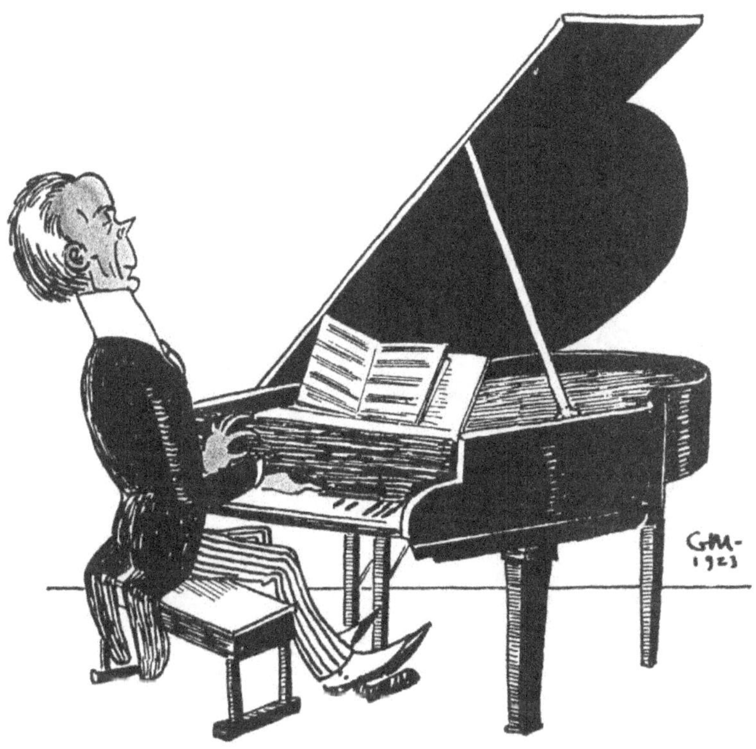

Mr. John Allen Carpenter composes a symphony.

Charles Collins

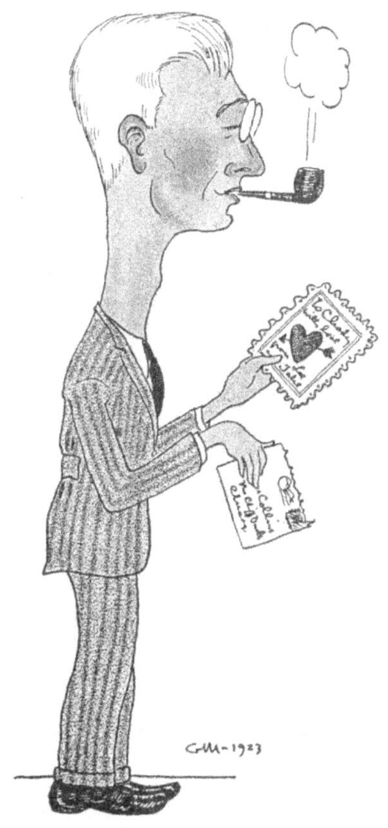

Mr. Charles Collins receives a valentine from the Messrs. Shubert.

Clarence Darrow

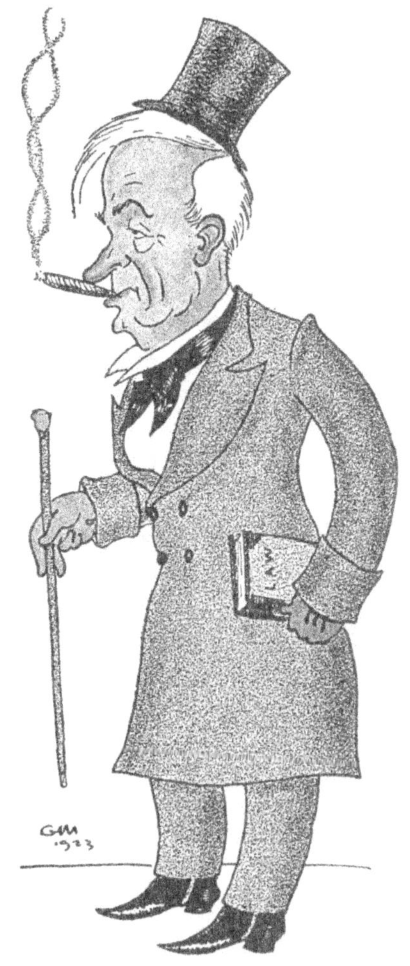

Mr. Clarence Darrow enters Court.

Philip Richard Davis and Wallace Rice

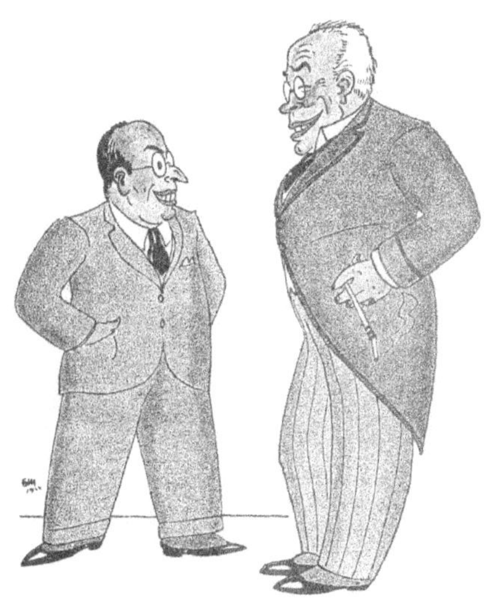

Mr. Philardee Davis and Mr. Wallace Rice
recall some sonnet they have written.

William Emmett Dever

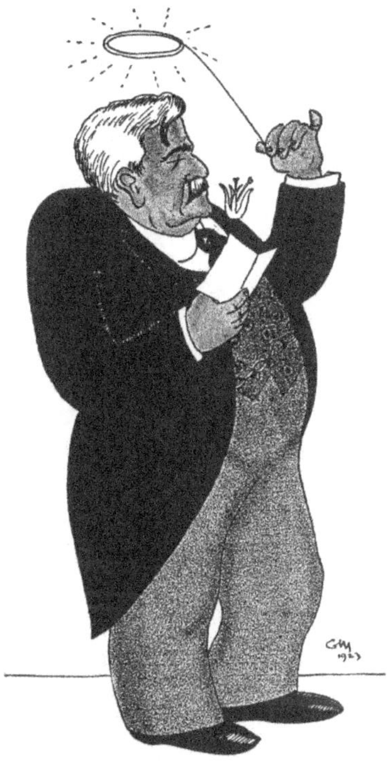

Mayor Dever receives a vote of thanks from the Oak Park Volstead Society.

Frederick Donaghey

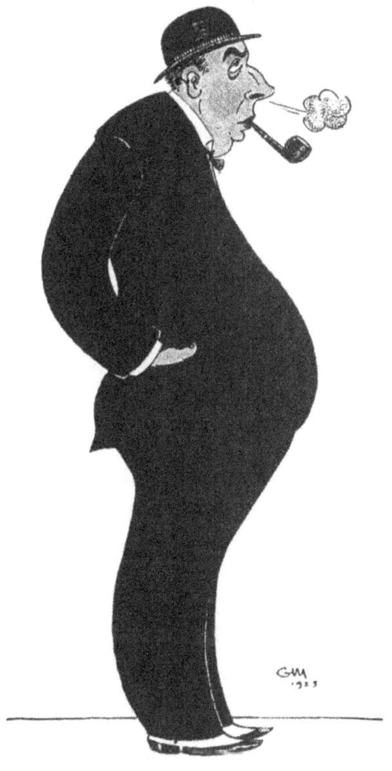

*Mr. Frederick Donaghey ponders a quotation
from Plato to qualify a Shubert show.*

Charles Erbstein

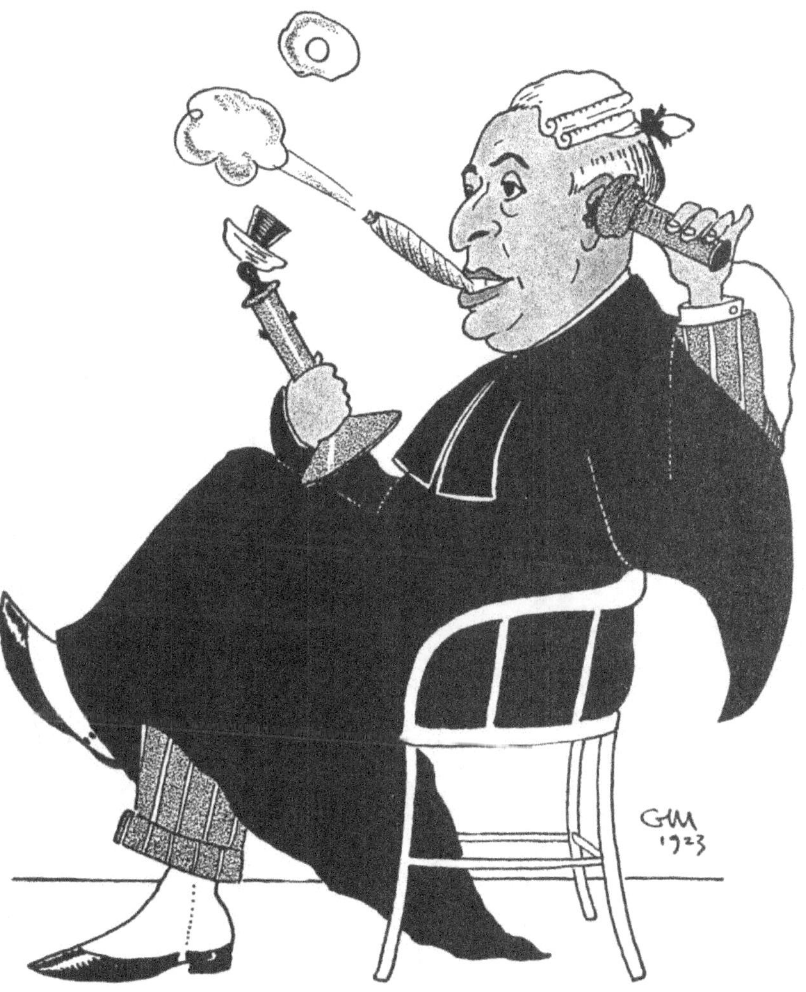

Mr. Charles Erbstein sitting in chambers.

Kellogg Fairbank

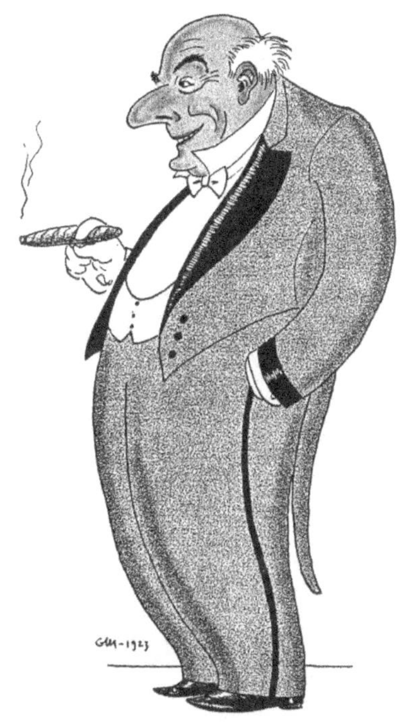

Mr. Kellogg Fairbank.

Morris Fishbein and Carl B. Roden

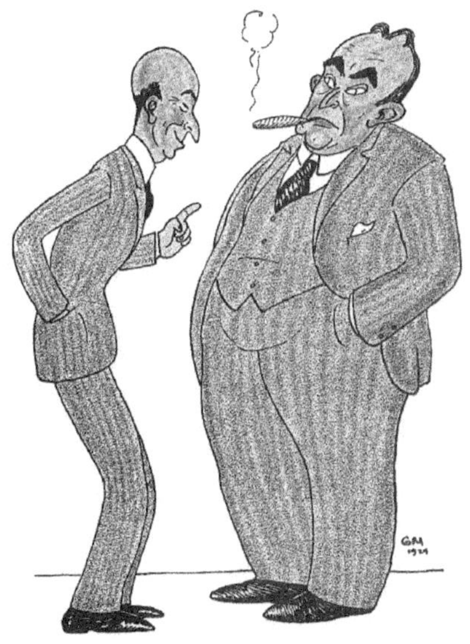

Dr. Morris Fishbein and Mr. Carl B. Roden
discuss the medical works of Ben Hecht.

Henry B. Fuller

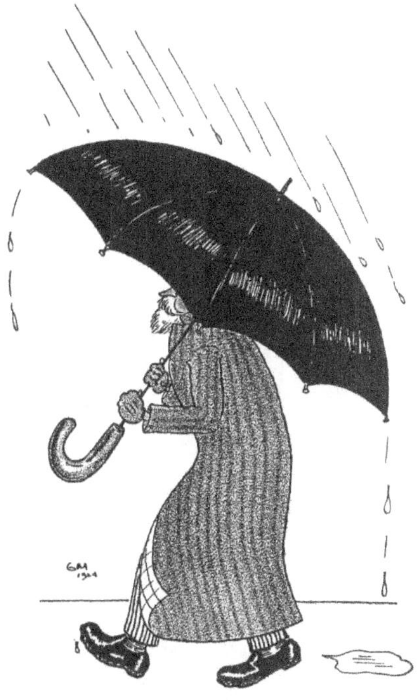

Mr. Henry B. Fuller ventures forth from a promenade.

O. L. Hall

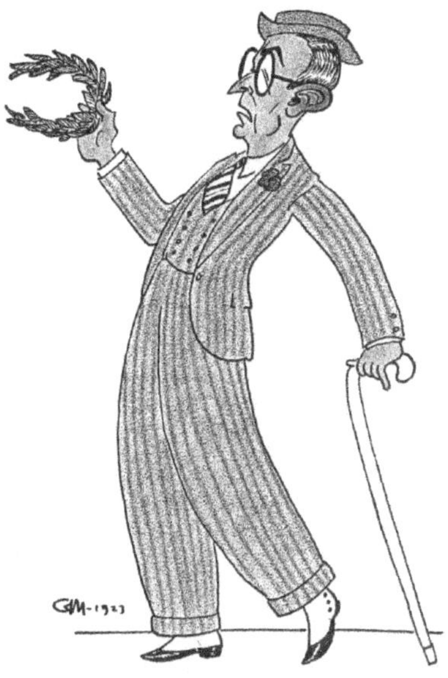

Dr. O. L. Hall places a wreath of poison-ivy upon the altar of Thespis.

Harry Hansen

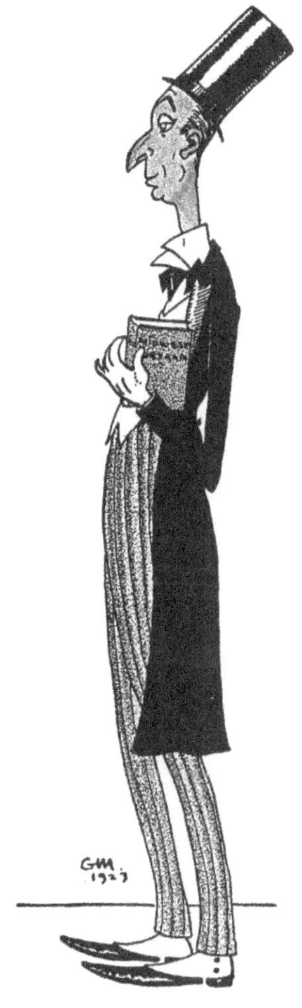

Dr. Harry Hansen surveys the Middle West from a table at Scholgl's.

Karl Edwin Harriman

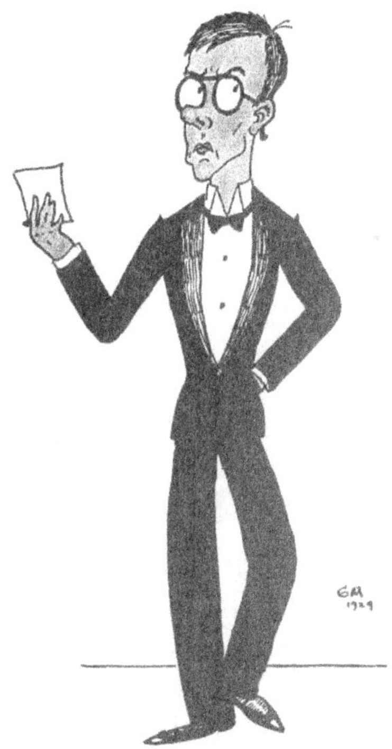

*Mr. Karl Edwin Harriman reads a paper
before the Chicago Literary Club.*

Ben Hecht

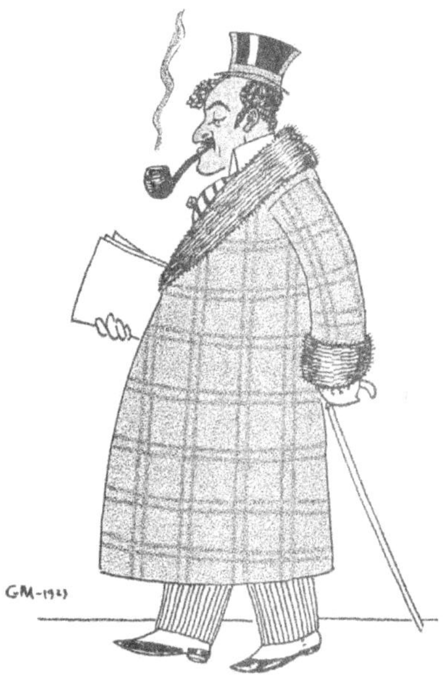

Mr. Ben Hecht completes a series of bed-time stories for The Youth's Companion.

Louis Houseman and Guy Hardy

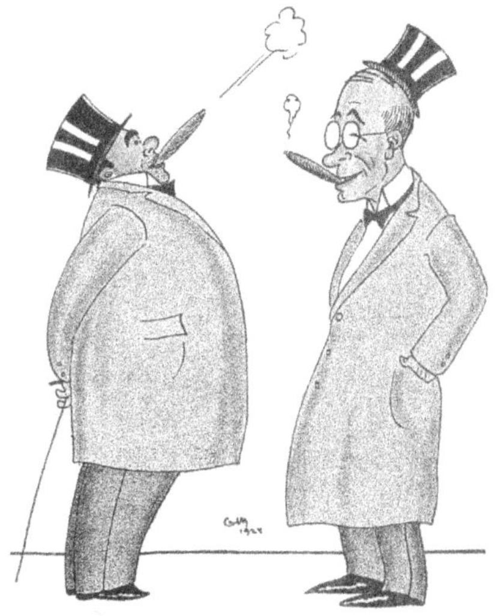

Mr. Lou Houseman and Mr. Guy Hardy confer on the theatrical situation.

Samuel Insull

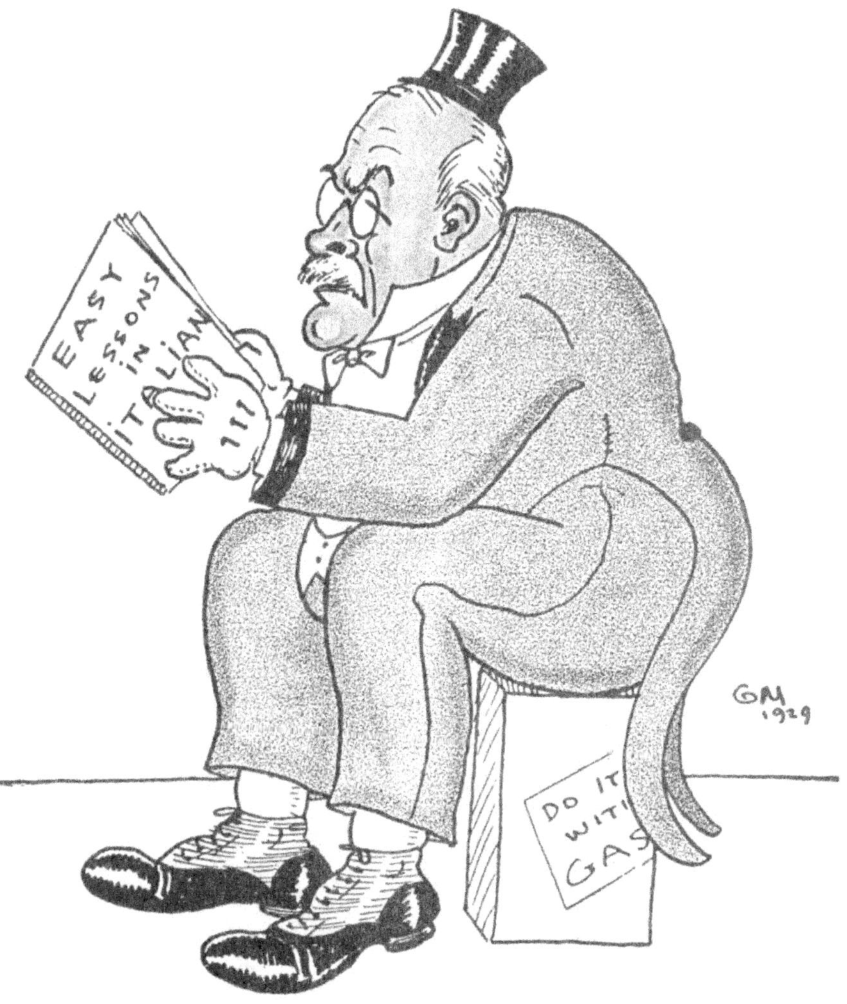

Mr. Samuel Insull makes a public utility of the opera.

Llewellyn Jones

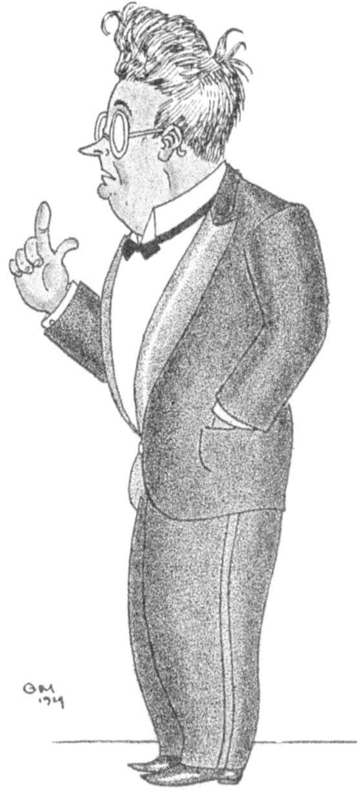

Dr. Llewellyn Jones attends a "Bookfellows" dinner.

J. U. Nicolson

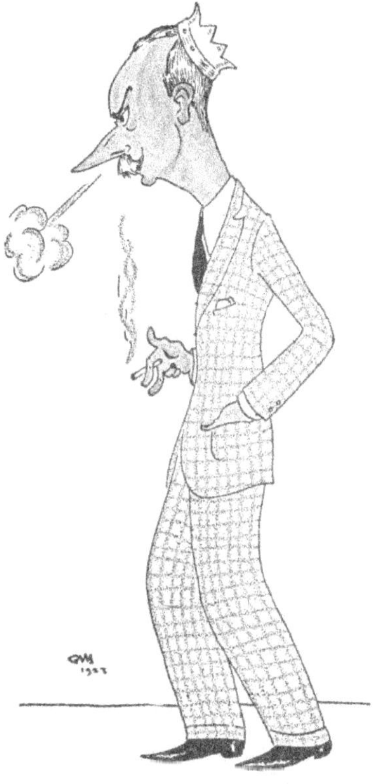

The King of the Black Isles [J. U. Nicolson].

Adolph Kroch

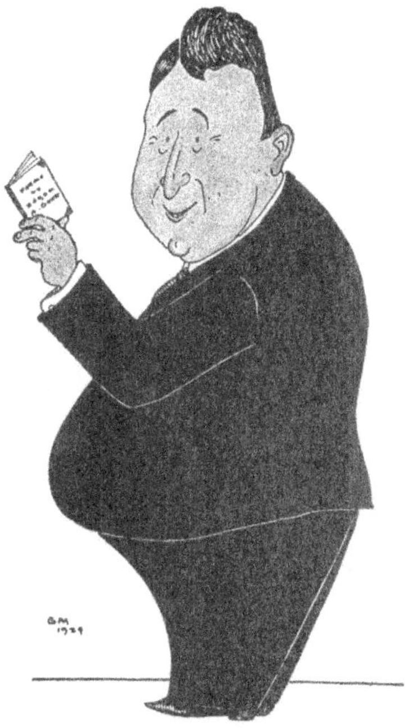

Mr. A. Kroch receives a book for Christmas.

Victor Lawson

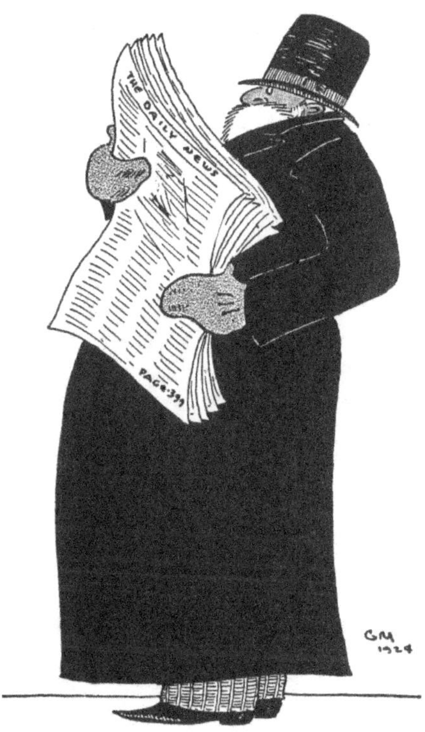

Mr. Victor Lawson trying to find one of his own editorials among the pages of The Daily News.

J. Hamilton Lewis

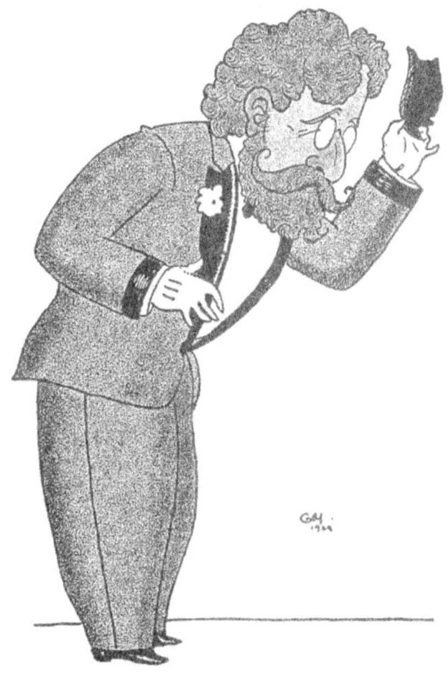

Senator J. Hamilton Lewis forgets the moment that he is not a candidate.

James Weber Linn

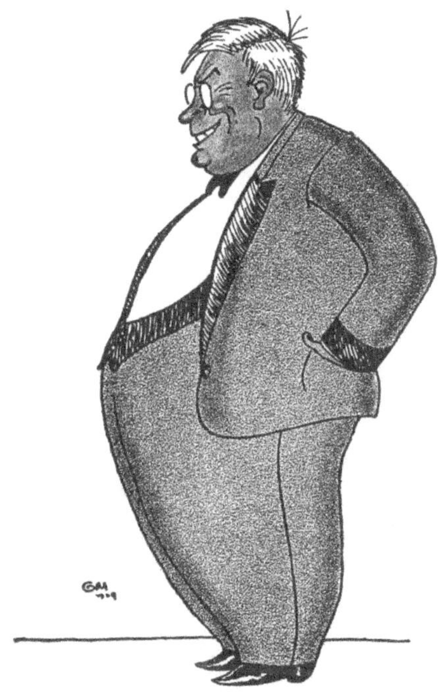

*Professor James Weber Linn pulls a literary nifty
before the ladies' Pre-Raphaelite Circle of Englewood.*

Richard Henry Little

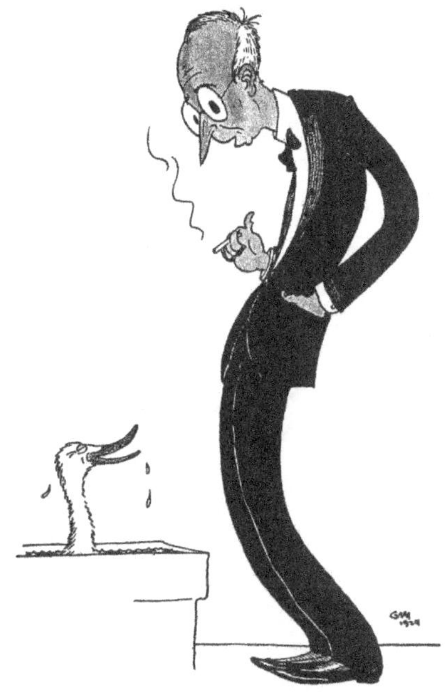

Mr. Richard Henry Little interrogates Leda, the somnambulant swan, at the Chez Pierre.

Allister McCormick

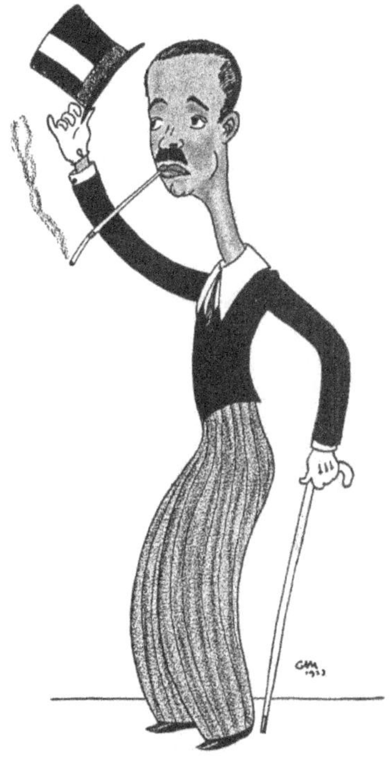

Mr. Allister McCormick returns.

Harold McCormick

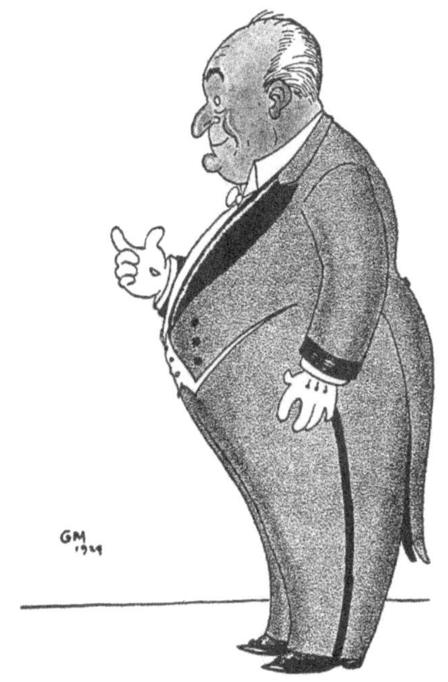

Mr. Harold McCormick.

Frederick McLaughlin

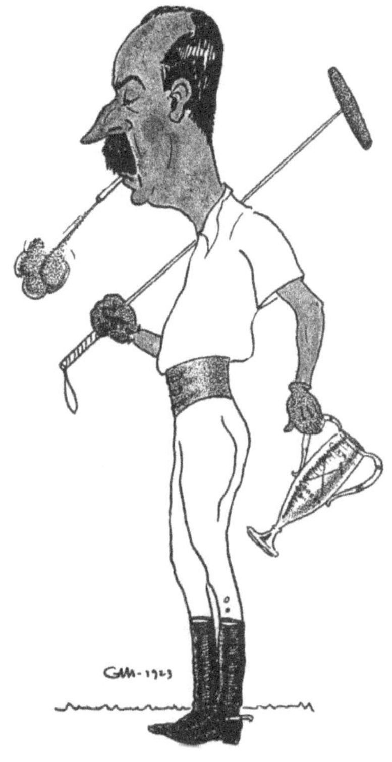

Maj. Frederick McLaughlin retires from polo.

Eames McVeagh

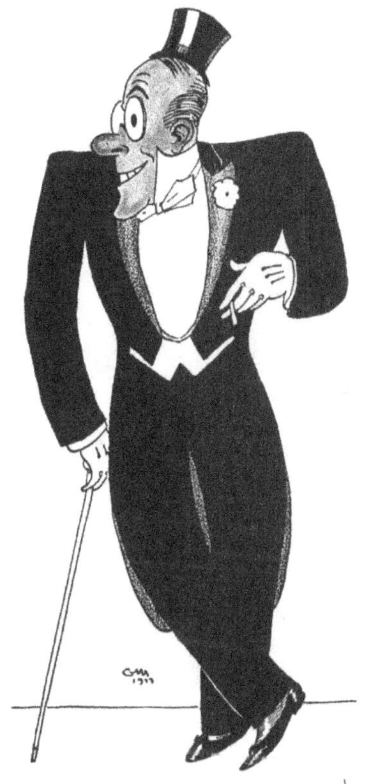

Mr. Eames McVeagh graces the opera.

Edgar Lee Masters

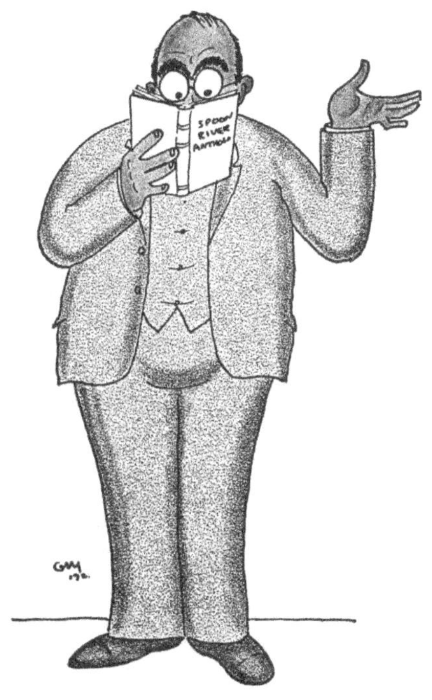

Mr. Edgar Lee Masters reads aloud from his own works.

Count Minotto

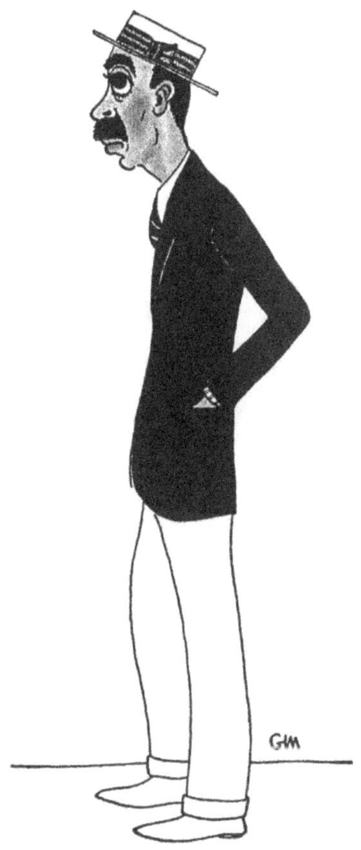

Count Minotto looking 'em over.

Murray Nelson and Arthur Bissell

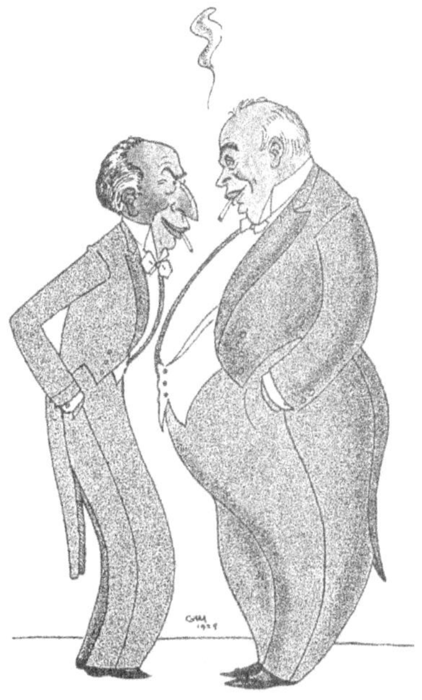

*Mr. Murray Nelson and Mr. Arthur Bissell
discuss the Ancien Régime of Chicago's Beau Monde.*

Howard Vincent O'Brien

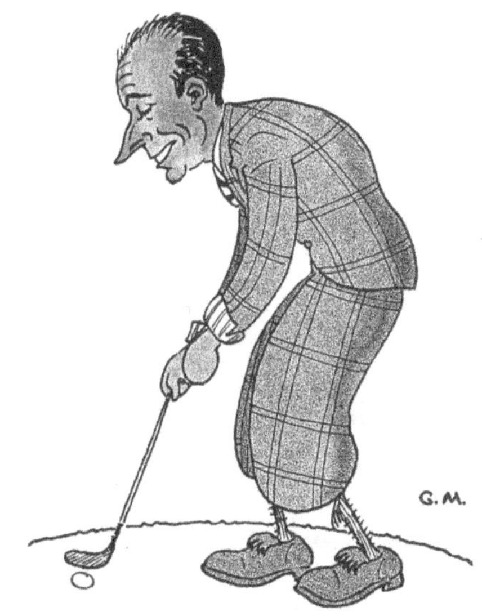

Mr. Howard Vincent O'Brien at Indian Hill.

Joseph Medill Patterson and Robert Rutherford McCormick

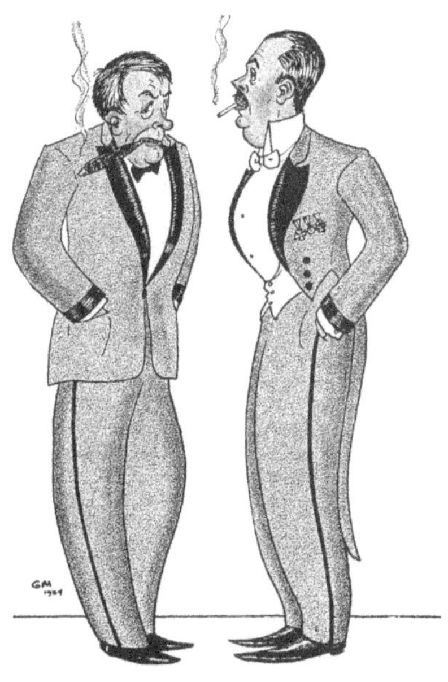

Captain J. M. Patterson and Colonel R. R. McCormick contrive a military editorial for The Chicago Tribune.

Keith Preston

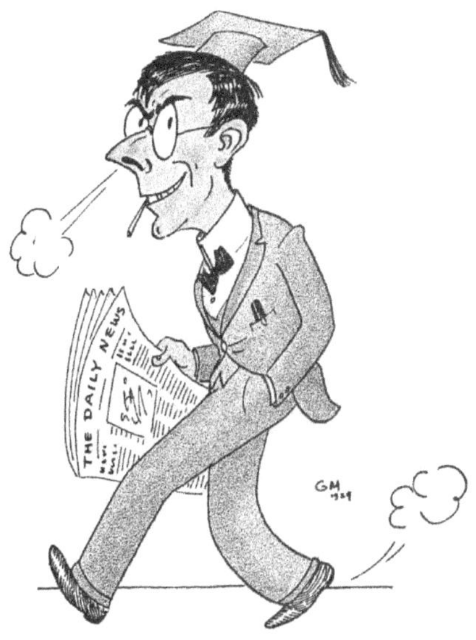

Dr. Keith Preston quits the campus for a window in Wells Street.

Georgio Polacco

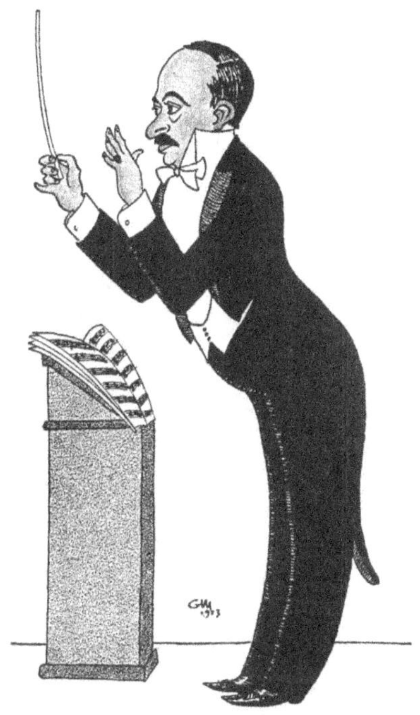

Maestro Georgio Polacco.

George Buckley, Harry Ridings and John Garrity

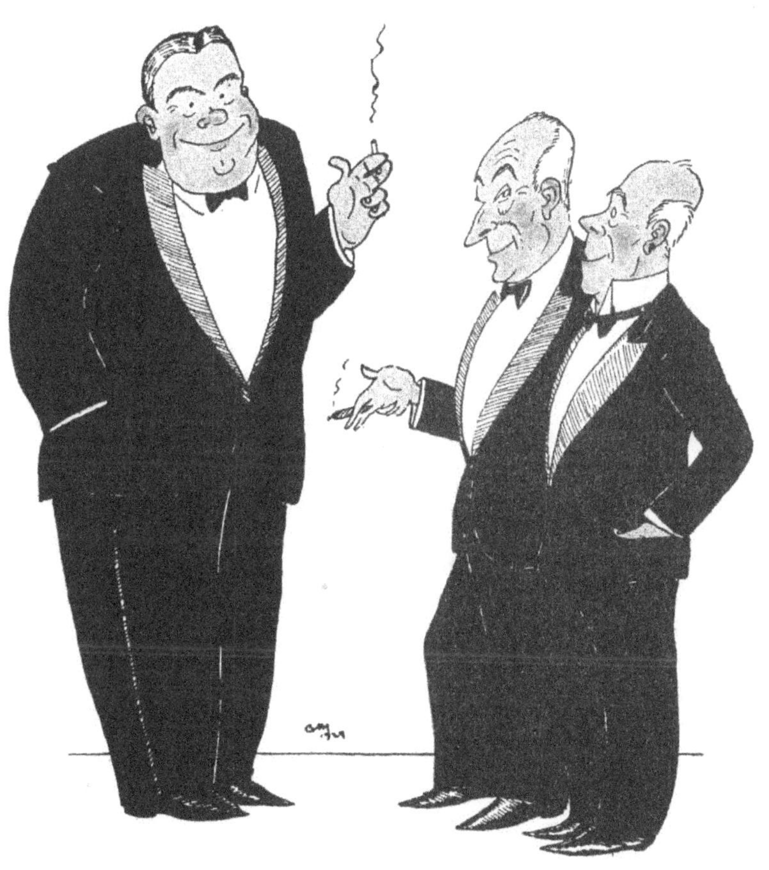

AT ANY FIRST NIGHT: Mr. George Buckley,
Mr. Harry Ridings and Mr. John Garrity.

Carl Sandburg

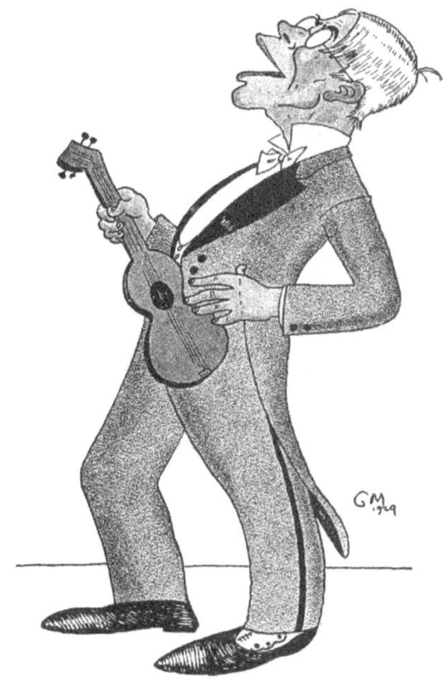

Mr. Carl Sandburg singing "Frankie and Johnny"
at the Fourth Baptist Church in Evanston.

Lew Sarett and William Ramsay

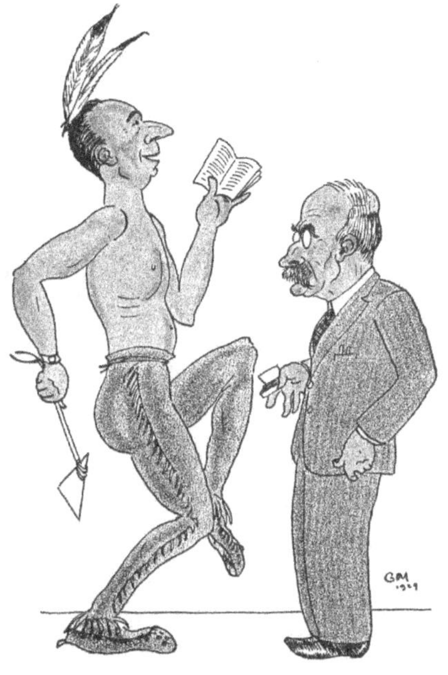

Mr. Lew Sarett and Professor William Ramsay
concern themselves with the various aspects of the ars poetica.

John C. Schaffer

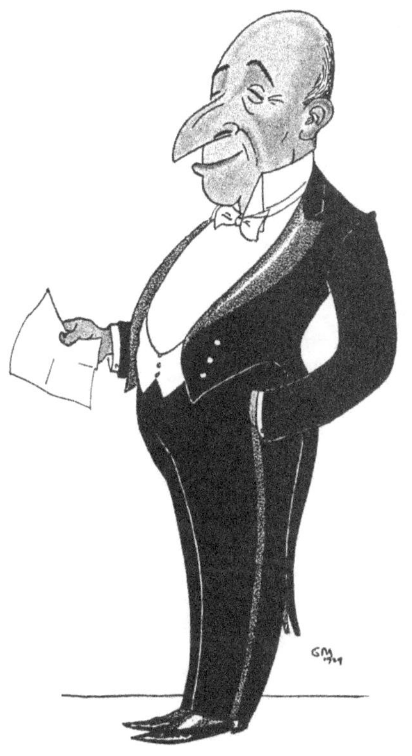

Mr. John C. Schaffer learns that The Evening Post has three new subscribers.

Howard Shaw

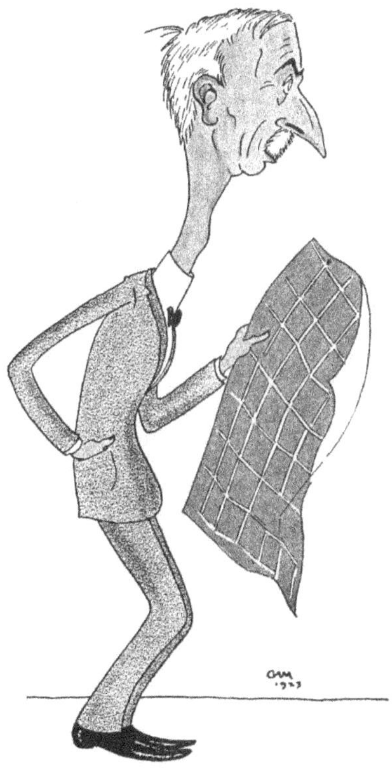

Mr. Howard Shaw glances over the plans for the new zoo.

Henry Justin Smith

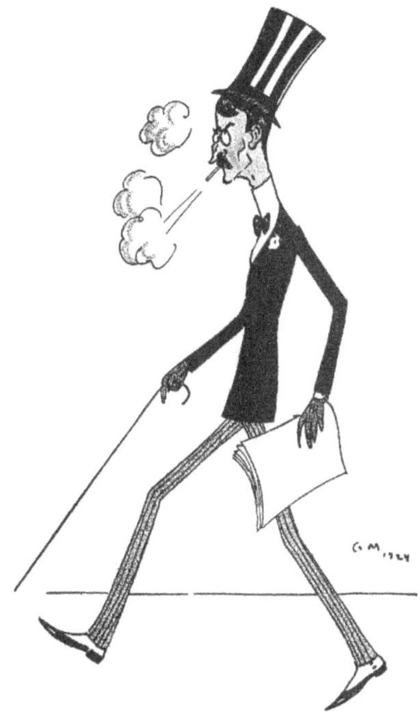

Mr. Henry Justin Smith saunters down Wells Street
with the manuscript of a new novel.

Wallace Smith

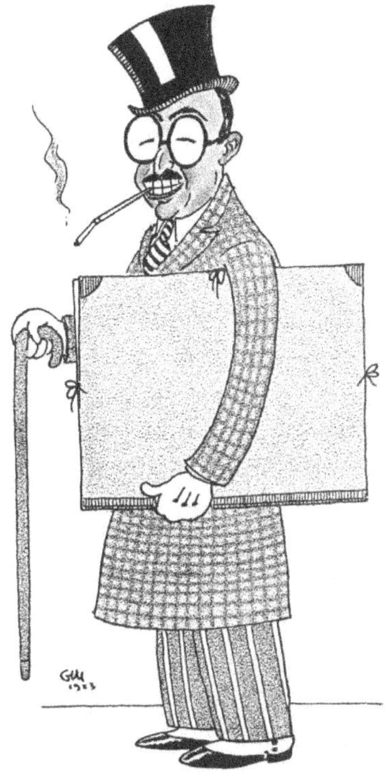

Mr. Wallace Smith shows a few drawings to the District Attorney.

Vincent Starrett

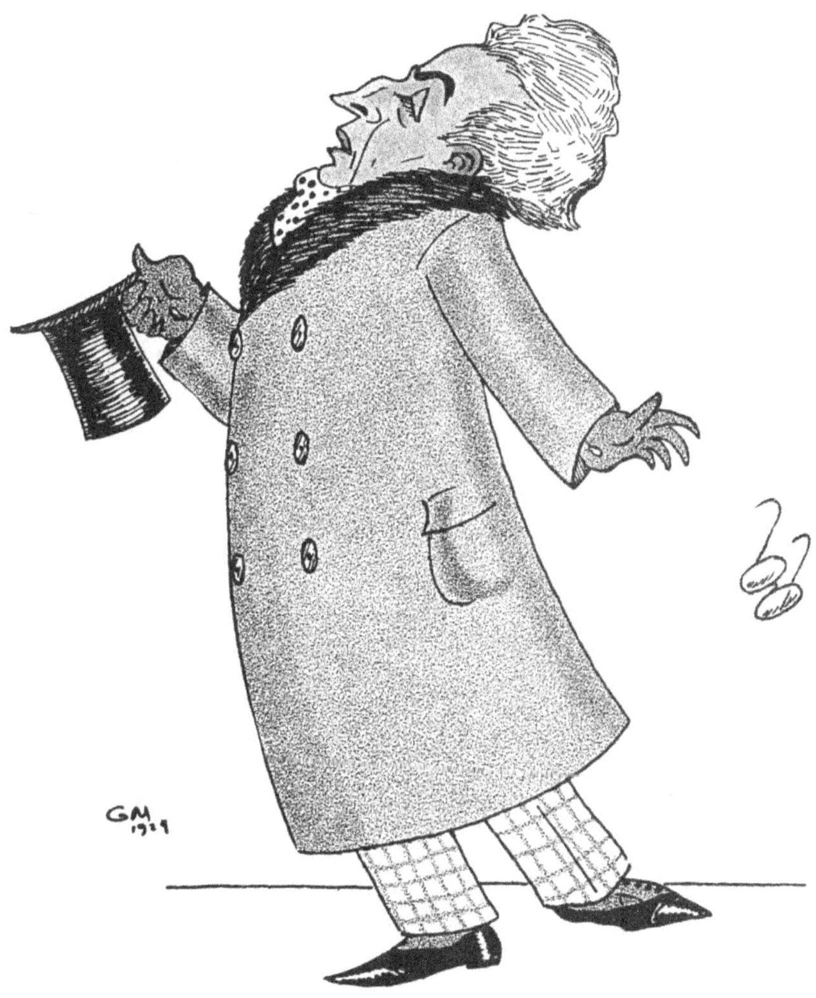

Mr. Vincent Starrett, after witnessing a performance of "The Fool," throws away his spectacles.

Vilhjalmur Stefansson

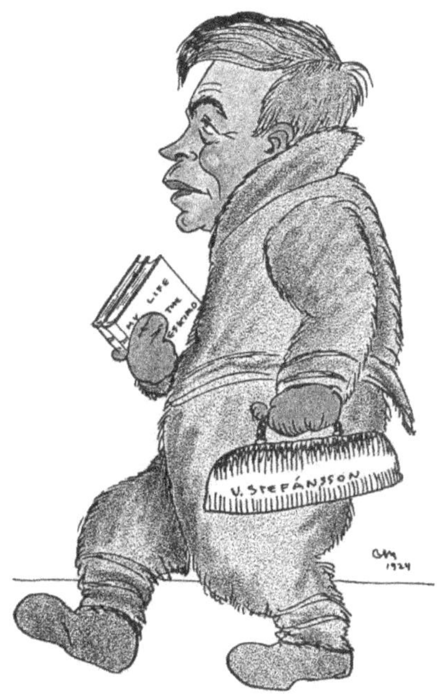

Mr. Vilhjalmur Stefansson blows down from the North.

Ashton Stevens

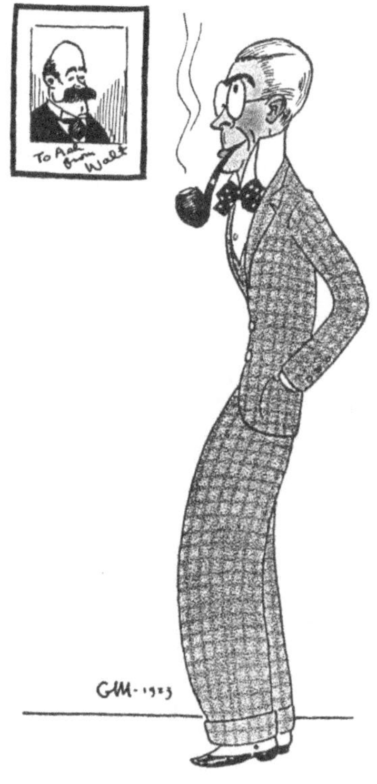

Mr. Ashton Stevens contemplates a portrait of the late Walter Pater.

Frederick Stock

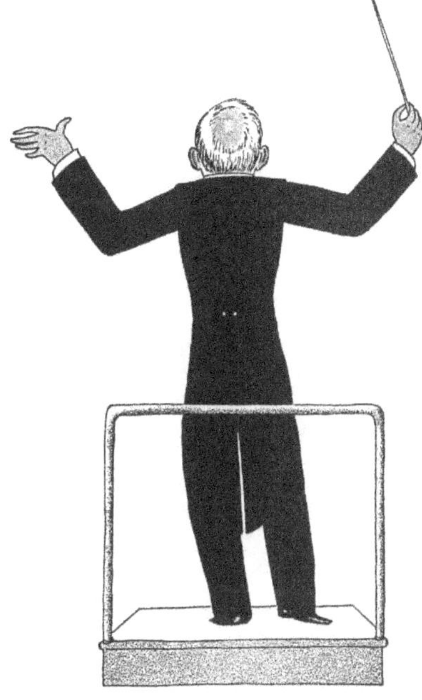

Mr. Frederick Stock.

Lorado Taft

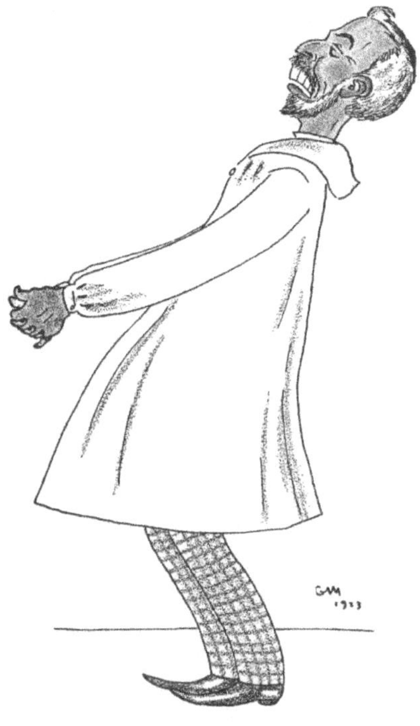

Mr. Lorado Taft beholding a vision of Chicago — the City Beautiful.

Thomas Tallmadge and John Norton

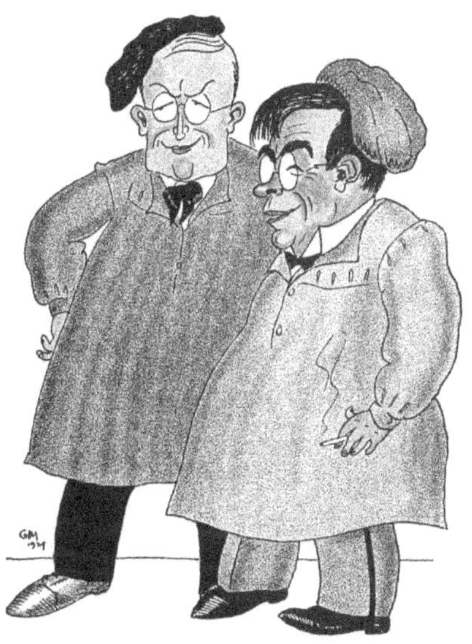

Mr. Thomas Tallmadge and Mr. John Norton
bring Bohemia to the Tree Studios.

Hobart Chatfield Chatfield-Taylor

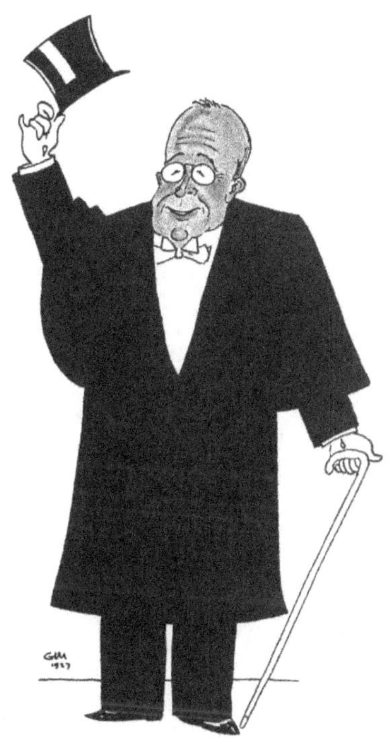

Mr. Hobart Chatfield Chatfield-Taylor returns to Michigan Boulevard.

Henry Kitchell Webster

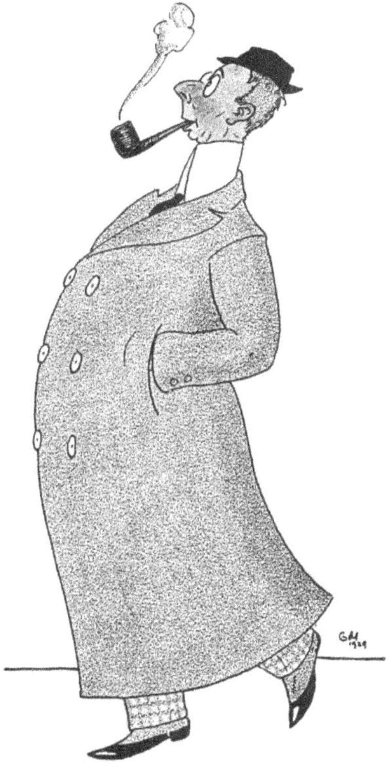

Mr. Henry Kitchell Webster considers writing the words for a new "Schubert Serenade" to be dedicated to Lee and Jake.

Benjamin Marshall

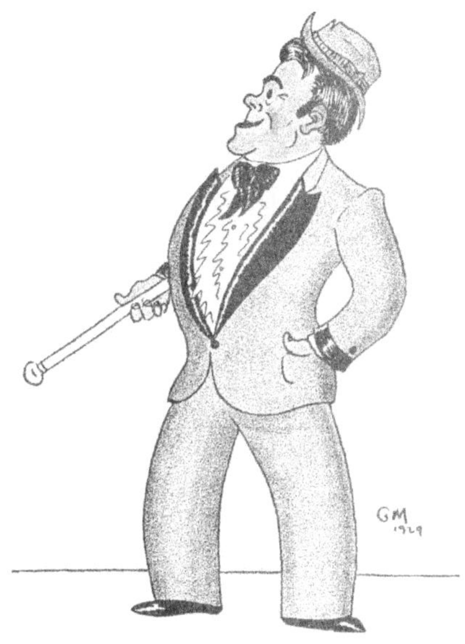

Mr. Benjamin Marshall attends a first night.